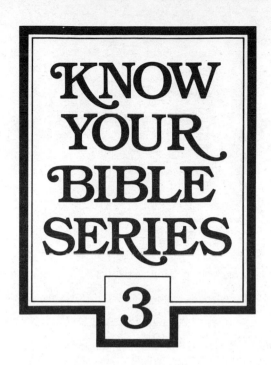

KNOW YOUR BIBLE SERIES

3

DEUTERONOMY
ZEPHANIAH
NAHUM
HABAKKUK
JEREMIAH
LAMENTATIONS

ROY L. SMITH

ABINGDON PRESS
NASHVILLE

Deuteronomy, Zephaniah, Nahum, Habakkuk, Jeremiah, Lamentations

No. 209145
Printed in U.S.A.

INTRODUCTION

The Old Testament prophets, if they could arise from their tombs and speak, would probably agree with the wag who once said, "Lord, deliver me from my friends; I can take care of my enemies myself!"

Few religious thinkers have suffered more at the hands of well-intentioned and devoted interpreters than these great pioneers of faith who preached to the Hebrews in God's behalf hundreds of years before he made the perfect revelation of himself in Jesus Christ. Their plain words have been twisted out of all semblance to their original meaning in order to make them support weird theories and strange doctrines. Their fundamental teachings have been ignored because they do not fit into the artificial "plan of salvation" invented by some cultist. The tremendous social and economic facts with which they struggled have been overlooked because they do not seem to be "spiritual."

The Hebrew prophets did not live in a vacuum, nor did they breathe the rarefied air of some exalted plane of existence far removed from the grim facts of real life. Rather, they labored in the midst of events and movements of earth-shaking significance. They watched social, political, and economic changes take place which revolutionized the whole manner of life for the plain man on the street. They saw the ancestral faith in God undermined by "practical politicians" and "religious realists" and protested against the secularizing influences with all the powers at their command.

At all times the Old Testament prophets were endeavoring to alleviate the harsh conditions under which they were compelled to live. In doing so it was impossible to ignore or evade social and economic facts, for they were dreadful evils which contributed to the spiritual impoverishment of the people. As a consequence the prophets dealt vigorously with such questions as land grabbing, judicial corruption, and political knavery. There could be no salvation for the plain people of Judah which remained indifferent to the subject of taxes.

The prophets of this period were compelled to do their work under the suspicious eyes of dictators holding the power of life and death over people and nations. Through at least a half a century (696-642 B.C.) they were driven underground by an

3

ancient puppet regime which hounded them and harried them in the effort to appease foreign overlords who were both pagan and callous. But in spite of persecutions and martyrdoms they kept the flame of faith burning.

It should be of the greatest inspiration to we who live in fear of seeing the most precious achievements of civilization go down under the bombs to remember that some of the boldest words spoken in God's behalf were uttered by the prophets during the worst days Judah had ever known. Nothing emerges from a study of the Old Testament prophets in plainer terms than this—the voice of God can be heard during the worst times.

True, the people through whom God is compelled to speak are not all saints of the highest order. It is often necessary for the devout person to listen with great care and judge with great discrimination, but even in Zephaniah's cry of terror and Nahum's narrow nationalism there is an accent that is from God. On the other hand, Habakkuk and Jeremiah saw just as much terror and suffered just as much as anyone known to history; but their faith has lighted hundreds of centuries since their day, and no darkness will ever put it out.

There is nothing in the background or the environment of these ancient preachers which explains them. They came out of the unknown, spoke their word for God, and went on to join the immortals. But their words have lived because "the Spirit of the Lord" was upon them.

Among those who listened to them were kings, governors, judges, bankers, landlords, and capitalists. Likewise they preached to the humble and the poor—rural shepherds, dirt farmers, debtors, and the expropriated. "Right wingers" and "leftists" were in their audiences, as were also the grafters, the politicians, and the corruptionists. Orthodoxy fought them, time-serving priests hated them, and prophets who preached for pay denounced them. But with one supreme loyalty in their lives—their confidence that they spoke for God—they went their lonely way and delivered their unpopular messages.

ROY L. SMITH

4

Writing Scripture Under Dictators

1 ## What period of Hebrew history are we to study?

One hundred and fifteen years of unrelieved tragedy!
Israel, the larger of the two Hebrew kingdoms, passed out of
existence when its capital, Samaria, was destroyed by the
Assyrians under the leadership of Sargon in 721 B.C., and just
twenty years later Judah, the smaller of the two states, barely
missed a similar fate when its capital, Jerusalem, was beseiged
by an Assyrian host under the personal command of the
emperor, Sennacherib. An indemnity, which included practically everything of value in the city, slaked the greed of the
invader for the moment; but it was only the first in a long series
of annual payments which, during the course of the century
that followed, bled the little nation white. In the year 586 B.C.,
following an uprising on the part of the frantic people,
Jerusalem was completely destroyed by the Babylonians under
Nebuchadrezzar, whereupon the kingdom came to an inglori-
ous end.

During that period of one hundred and fifteen years the tiny
Palestinian states passed through one horror after another.
Intrigue was in the air, and the highways of the East were filled
with envoys bent on political missions of dubious honesty.
Empires rose and fell. Whole nations were carried off into
captivity and passed forever from the scene of history.
Barbarian hordes, sweeping down from the north, threatened
the whole of civilization. The mastery of the world changed
hands. Fear stalked the earth. It is doubtful if ever in all the
history of the world up to that time so many people had suffered
so severely as during that century. Yet out of that welter of woe
six complete books, besides some poems and other fragments,
emerged to take their place eventually in our Bible.

2 ## What scripture was produced during this period?

The bulk of the book of Deuteronomy (chapters five to
twenty-six and twenty-eight); four prophets (Zephaniah,
Nahum, Habakkuk, Jeremiah); and a collection of exquisite,

5

though heartbreaking, poems called Lamentations. In addition, a beginning was made on the books of Kings and some Psalms were composed.

3 How did the period open?

When Sennacherib turned back to re-establish order in his realm in 701 B.C., having extorted an indemnity from Jerusalem which stripped the city of practically everything of value, he left behind him a nation that was utterly exhausted. Worse than its impoverishment was its disillusionment. Certain religious reforms, initiated by Hezekiah under pressure from the prophetic party, were held responsible for the nation's disaster, and the people entered into their century of sorrow bitter and sullen, ready to embrace almost any religious faith that offered the slightest hope. In the course of the next one hundred and fifteen years the nation passed through at least five major crises.

4 What were these five crises?

1. The reactionary reign of Manasseh, 696-642 B.C.
2. The Scythian invasion, 630-625 B.C.
3. The fall of Nineveh, 612 B.C., and the rise of the Babylonian Empire.
4. The first Babylonian invasion, 598-597 B.C.
5. The second Babylonian invasion and the destruction of Jerusalem, 587-586 B.C.

5 What about the reactionary reign of Manasseh?

It is impossible to understand the significance of the reign of Manasseh without knowing something about the prophetic party to which reference was made in Question No. 3. It will be remembered from Study No. 2 that Isaiah became discouraged in his efforts to influence the policy of the government at the time of the Syro-Israelite crisis in 734 B.C. (II Kings 15:25-30; 16:1-19; Isaiah 7), and that he transferred his hopes of the salvation of the kingdom to a little band of disciples. These he trained with great care, inculcating in them the exalted principles of righteousness, justice, and morality which he preached (Isaiah 8:16-20).

The prophetic party was responsible for some far-reaching reforms which were undertaken during the later years of

Hezekiah's reign, and when the Assyrian disaster fell upon the nation with its crushing load of tribute the pro-pagan elements were quick to lay the blame for all the nation's woes at the feet of the Yahweh group. When Manasseh came to the throne in 696 B.C., at the age of twelve years, the discontented elements made effective use of their opportunity and persuaded the young monarch that his father's devotion to Yahweh and the prophetic party had resulted in disaster. The one wise and reasonable course, they argued, was to embrace the pagan faith of the Assyrians, worship their gods, and seek prosperity for the nation through collaboration with its overlord. Thereupon began the most pagan period in Hebrew history.

6 What was the program of the prophetic party?

In broad terms it may be said that there were three planks in their platform: (1) In season and out they insisted upon the worship of Yahweh, divorced from all admixtures of paganism and divested of all heathen rites. In time this took the form of a demand that all worship should be centralized in the Temple at Jerusalem, with the rural altars and shrines destroyed. (2) Loyal to the ancient ideals of *mishpat* (simple social justice), in which the nation had been instructed by Moses in the desert, the prophetic party met every change in social and economic life with the demand that the rights of individual Hebrews, including the poorest and humblest, should be respected as a part of the ancient religious faith and protected as a major purpose of the government. In this they were inspired of course by the teachings of the great writing prophets of the eighth century, Amos, Hosea, Isaiah, Micah. (3) Their political policy was simple—"no entangling alliances." In every crisis they insisted that the government should pursue a neutral course so far as that was possible. This, in turn, was a direct outgrowth of their religious faith, a product of the belief that Yahweh was the God of the Hebrews, sworn to protect them against all foes. Any political alliance with a pagan nation, in the opinion of the prophetic party, was a concession to the pagan gods which they were altogether unwilling to make.

7 What were the reforms inaugurated during Hezekiah's reign?

By order of the king the Temple was purged of its pagan altars

(II Chronicles 30:14), and the rural high places were destroyed (II Kings 18:4). All this was done with the thought that the worship of Yahweh would be purged of its pagan elements.

8 What were the "high places"?

When the Hebrews entered the Land of Promise from the desert they found the Canaanites worshiping their Baalim (plural of Baal, which is the name used for the local god) at numerous shrines scattered throughout the country. Some of these sanctuaries had been in use for many generations and were highly venerated. In some cases they were elaborate establishments with houses for the priests and "sacred prostitutes" and great outdoor altars. In other cases they were no more than crude little establishments attended by solitary priests who lived off the sacrifices of the near-by villagers. In still other instances they were only spots in the midst of fields, set aside for the purpose of offering prayers and sacrifices in behalf of good crops.

As they were usually situated atop some hill, they came to be known as "high places." Originally they were dedicated to the Baal of the neighborhood, but as the Hebrews mingled with the Canaanites at these "high places" the worship became a blend of Yahwehism and paganism. Because the priests who presided over the shrines were considerably removed from the Temple at Jerusalem and any official control, it was easy for the worship at these rural altars to be adapted to the whims and preferences of the worshipers; and as a consequence the services were seriously corrupted.

But at least the "high places" had one merit—they were close to the people and served an important function in everyday life which has been overlooked by most Bible students.

9 What practical purpose did they serve?

According to the belief of the Hebrews, in common with most of the peoples of the ancient East, life depended upon the blood. They had noticed a dead body does not bleed. They concluded from this evidence that life resided in the blood. In the belief that life itself was given by the gods, they thought that the blood was sacred to the gods, and must not be used by men in any way. When they sacrificed animals on the altars the ritual back to the gods as the first act. Any animals to be killed for food had to be taken to the shrine and slaughtered there, that the blood might be returned to the god who had given the life. All this killing, being a part of a religious ritual, had to be performed by the priest, with the result that those who presided at these "high places" became the local butchers as well as the religious mediators for the people.

10 What objections did the prophets make?

They condemned the "high places" on three grounds. In the first place, as the local shrines had been dedicated originally to the worship of the local Baals, it was inevitable that remnants of paganism would be carried over into the worship of Yahweh to corrupt it in various ways. In the second place, the "high places" were centers for the practice of immoral acts which the prophets could not tolerate. In the third place, they perpetuated the worship of the Baals, which was in opposition to the Hebrew doctrines of *mishpat*. The prophetic party was convinced that there was no hope of improving the lot of the poor people so long as the worship of Baal, with its approval of social injustices, was permitted. The basis of the opposition, then, was religious, social, and economic.

11 How did Hezekiah's reforms come out?

To many a provincial zealot the destruction of the "high places" amounted to little less than sacrilege and an unwarranted interference in the life of the people. But as long as Hezekiah was able to maintain some political success his religious reforms were accepted. The king was a devout man by nature, and Isaiah exercised a great influence over him; but the prophet, being a city man and a member of the aristocracy which made Jerusalem its headquarters, was never able to carry the rural districts, even though he spoke out vigorously in behalf of justice for the country landowners on many occasions. It was pressure from the farmers and shepherds who bore the heavy burden of taxes which forced Hezekiah into the ill-fated revolt against Assyria (II Kings 18:7) and which, in turn, brought down upon the unhappy little land the terrible wrath of the Empire. This was the greatest disaster that had ever befallen Judah (II Kings 18:13-16), and it was interpreted as evidence that

Hezekiah's reforms were unpopular with Yahweh. As a consequence the king's last days were filled with anxiety. His land was seething with unrest; year by year the caravans loaded with tribute streamed out across the desert toward the great metropolis of Nineveh, capital of Assyria. The fact that Jerusalem had been saved, its walls left standing, and its Temple unviolated, impressed the king and the wealthy aristocrats. They were convinced that Isaiah was correct. But the rural villages having been sacked and the countryside despoiled and devastated, the farmers and shepherds were unimpressed by the preaching of the prophetic party. They were ready for just such a change in politics and religion as was ushered in under Manasseh, Hezekiah's twelve-year-old son who followed him to the throne.

12 Who was Manasseh?

Mounting the throne of Judah at the age of twelve (696 B.C.), Hezekiah's son and successor, Manasseh, inaugurated a reign of fifty-four years (696-642 B.C.), which, for length and reactionary paganism, was never equalled in Hebrew history. The explanation is very simple.

13 What is the explanation of Manasseh's reactionary reign?

The new king was only a child when he began to reign. His little kingdom had just come through a terrible experience which had shaken the life of the people to the foundations, and forces were at work which called for the utmost in administrative skill and political and moral sagacity. Manasseh had none of these.

The first fact the young monarch had to face was the cruel demands of Assyria. In addition to the normal expenses of government, the annual tribute absorbed everything the little land could produce over and above a bare living.

The second fact was the system by which the tribute was collected from the people. The government, being located in Jerusalem, had gathered about it the rich and powerful citizens of the land, to whom were delegated the various offices and responsibilities. To them there fell that task of collecting the money for the support of the government of Judah, and *in addition* the goods to be shipped to Nineveh. Each year enough had to be wrung out of the farmers and shepherds to pay the tribute, and to pay the aristocrats *their profit as middlemen-collectors*.

The third fact was the effect of this system. The total wealth and national resources of the little kingdom began to accumulate in the hands of the rich aristocrats. An army of collectors, court officials, strong-arm men (*gibborim*) swarmed the land. Poor farmers unable to meet their taxes were compelled to borrow from the Jerusalem moneylenders; and when the loans came due the courts, in league with the lenders, devised legal processes by which the land was seized by the creditors.

The fourth fact was closely allied with the third. According to the *mishpat* taught by Yahwehism, the ownership of land was a gift direct from God. The land was not subject to sale, but was to be held in perpetuity. Baalistic teachings, on the other hand, approved the sale of land as a legitimate procedure. As a consequence there was a strong trend toward Baalism among the wealthy moneylenders, for that was the only way in which their land-grabbing could be made legal.

14 What was Manasseh's program?

The official religion of Judah was deliberately altered for the purpose of validating the economic program of the moneylenders. The king erected altars for Baal in Jerusalem (II Kings 21:3, 11) and gave official sanction to paganism, which it had never had before. In that, however, he was supported by the popular theology of the time, which assumed that the god of the conqueror was stronger than the god of the conquered. It must have seemed like wise discretion to embrace the religion and worship the gods of the Assyrians, for they had proved themselves superior to Yahweh on the field of battle. In abandoning Yahwehism Manasseh did three things: (1) he provided legal sanction for the exploitations of the "right-wing" aristocrats and moneylenders of Jerusalem; (2) he placated the Assyrians by adopting their gods; (3) he defied the prophetic party.

15 What did the prophetic party do?

There are those who believe the prophet Micah was still alive at this time and that his vigorous protests (Micah 6:1-7; 7) were aimed at Manasseh. But in addition there were other prophetic

11

leaders, whose names must remain forever unknown, who preached with all their power against the prevailing paganism (II Kings 21:10 ff.) and suffered grievously as a consequence. Apparently the prophets were the only ones in the kingdom who made any determined effort to stem the tide, protect the people, and maintain the ancient faith.

16 Did they have any success?

Manasseh, resentful at their interference, slew them without mercy (Jeremiah 2:30) in such numbers that Jerusalem was filled with blood from one end to the other (II Kings 21:16). Tradition has it that even Isaiah, honored and respected by Hezekiah, was sawn in two with a wooden saw during this period of persecution (see Hebrews 11:37), but of this there is no proof. It was a period of high-handed murders in which no doubt some of the more radical farmers and shepherds lost their lives and the prophetic leaders suffered relentless persecution.

17 What could the protesting prophets do?

There was little they could accomplish in the field of practical politics; but by meeting clandestinely, discussing events and policies, and thinking their problems through together they strengthened one another in the faith and gradually evolved a philosophy of life, politics, and religion which survived the sword and the tryant. The record is scanty. Great gaps have to be filled in. But we know that the prophetic party suffered much the same experience under Manasseh that the Christians suffered under Roman persecutions when they were driven into the catacombs. Then came the Scythian invasion.

18 What was the Scythian invasion?

No one seems to know exactly who the Scythians were, beyond the fact that they were a wild, barbarous people from the regions north of Assyria. They came pouring down out of the hinterland like some terrible lava flow, burning and blazing their way across the earth. There had been a time when the Palestinian world would have rejoiced to see any enemy break the power of Assyria, but terrible as had been its tyranny the frightfulness of the Scythian menace was worse.

Between the Hebrews and the barbarians there was absolutely nothing in common. The Scythians could not be appealed to on any grounds of mercy or honor; they knew nothing of justice, pity, or morality.

19 **When did the Scythian invasion occur?**

Assyria felt its force first; and for a period of twenty-eight years Assyrian plains, cities, and villages were ravaged by the invader. But the menace was acute in Palestine during only about five years (630-625 B.C.), shortly after the death of Manasseh.

20 **How did Judah suffer from the Scythians?**

Quite contrary to all expectations inside the little kingdom of Judah, the Scythians did not attack the Hebrew state. Aside from a few desultory raids along the western borders in which occasional villages suffered, they made no direct war, probably for the reason that nearly one hundred and fifty years of Assyrian vassalage left little loot to tempt them. Jerusalem was never besieged, but the city's life was completely disrupted; the nations was demoralized by fear; and the universal terror inspired at least one prophet (Zephaniah) to preach the prophetic doctrine that all the nation's woes were a direct result of the abandonment of Yahweh and his principles of *mishpat*.

21 **Who was the reigning monarch at the time?**

The reactionary administration of Manasseh came to a close in 642 B.C., and the bloody old pagan was succeeded on the throne by his son Amon; but a conspiracy inside the government resulted in his assassination after a little more than two years in power (639 B.C.), and he was succeeded by his son Josiah (639-608 B.C.), one of the most devout and enlightened kings Judah ever had.

22 **What about that conspiracy?**

The Assyrian Empire had been badly shaken by the Scythians and other foes, and its grip on the world of the East was fast weakening. Egypt was able, during the closing years of Manasseh's reign, to shake off the oppressor and establish its independence. In the general confusion and disorganization of the world Judah saw her chance to withhold the annual tribute for a few years, and the kingdom was a ferment of restlessness and rising hopes. This was the cue for the farmers and shepherds (*am ha'arets,* meaning "the people of the land"), who had suffered most under the Assyrian yoke and the crushing tax burdens that had been passed on to them by the "right-wing politicians" of Jerusalem. They therefore rioted and slaughtered the Baal politicians who had engineered the assassination of Amon (II Kings 21:24), and proceeded to put Josiah, his son, upon the throne.

23 What kind of king was Josiah?

The young king was probably devout by nature; but coming to the throne at the age of eight years, and surrounded by the rural nobles and landowners who had put him into power, it was perfectly natural that the early years of his reign should have been, in fact, a reflection of their views and policies. However, he must have been in sympathy with them, for Jeremiah, who was suspicious of all kings, paid him high tribute after his death (Jeremiah 22:15, 16) as a man who administered *mishpat* with vigor and impartiality as a loyal servant of Yahweh.

Economic wrongs and social injustices under which the rural landlords and farmers had suffered were ended. New judges were appointed for the courts and provided with new officials chosen because of their friendliness to the common people. Many farmers who had been dispossessed by the moneylenders of Manasseh's day regained their possessions and were confirmed in their title by the new government. The need for such reform is graphically portrayed by Zephaniah (3:1-3), the prophet of the time, who, with Jeremiah, added the sanction of the prophetic party to the official policy. Just when the reforms were at their height, and in need of official sanction of the highest authority, the "book of the law" was discovered in the Temple. But concerning this we will make a more careful inquiry a little later on.

24 How did Josiah's reign turn out?

The Scythian invasion demoralized the Assyrian Empire sufficiently that revolts sprang up with more or less success throughout the world. The Babylonians in the south, under the leadership of a Chaldean king, were especially successful. For a

14

time it appeared that the new Empire might be able to overthrow the old tyrant and usurp the mastery of the world as Assyria's successor.

An Egyptian army was hastening north to the aid of Assyria; and Josiah, king of Judah, went out to meet the Egyptian king at the field of Megiddo. It is not quite clear whether it was a friendly call designed as a courtesy, or a military gesture of defiance. But whatever it may have been, Josiah was slain by the Egyptian (II Kings 23:29-30) and his body was taken back to Jerusalem in the royal chariot for burial.

The faction that had put Josiah in power undertook to put one of his sons upon the throne in his place, but the Pharaoh of Egypt seized him, put him in chains, and carried him off to Egypt. Then choosing another of Josiah's sons (evidently known to have pro-Egyptian sympathies), he put him on the throne and assessed a tribute of something more than two millions of dollars against the poor little kingdom (II Kings 23:32-35). All this, together with powerful threats from the surrounding nations, produced an acute problem for the prophetic party.

25 What was the party's problem?

It appeared in two forms. First, why was the devout and faithful Josiah allowed to die in the midst of his reign of reform? If he was doing Yahweh's will, why was he not supported and protected in doing it?

In the second place, if the reforms launched by Josiah had the approval of Yahweh, why should the nation be allowed to suffer under the oppressions of other nations all about? When the prophetic party undertook to answer by saying that Judah was being punished for her sins, it was pointed out that the oppressors were even more sinful.

26 What was the solution of the problem?

There is no evidence that the prophetic party, as such, ever solved the problem, but there was a noble and high-minded prophet who wrestled with it about this time. In his efforts to think the matter through he produced one of the books of the Old Testament which is understood by very few people, but which is one of the most exalted and valuable books in the Old

Testament. Of Habakkuk we shall study a little later. Meanwhile we must inquire concerning Nineveh.

27 What was Nineveh?

Far up in the heart of Assyria, sprawling along the banks of the upper reaches of the Tigris River, lay the capital of the Empire—the city of Nineveh. By almost any standard it would have been called a great city—rich, powerful, vast, and in a certain sense cultured. Because it was the seat of the government of Assyria it frequently gave its name to the nation, and its fall was an event that shook the earth.

28 What about the fall of Nineveh?

For seven hundred years the peoples of the East had lived, in one way or another, under the shadow of Assyrian power. It was not always true that Assyria was oppressing them, but there was hardly a year from 1300 B.C. to 600 B.C. that the threat of Assyrian domination was not something to be reckoned with. For almost three centuries (875 B.C. to 600 B.C.) her armies constituted the greatest military machine of the world. By the middle of the seventh century B.C., in spite of the fact that it was beset by many weaknesses, the Assyrian Empire was the master of the East.

But the Scythian invasion administered a shock from which the Empire never recovered. The spirit of revolt seized the subject peoples, and the small nations prepared feverishly for any eventuality. As evidence of the increased spirit of defiance of all things Assyrian, the Hebrews tore down the pagan altars which had been erected in Jerusalem during the reign of Manasseh (II Chronicles 33:14-16). Then came the Medes, a hard-fighting race beyond the mountains on the eastern border of Assyria, hammering home deadly blows. The Babylonians opened a second front on the south. Within the space of a few months the mighty Empire was ringed about with foes, all stalking for the kill; and in 612 B.C. the once-proud capital fell to the invaders. Ashur-urballit, the Assyrian monarch, continued the struggle for a few futile years, but all the world knew that the dreaded tyrant had ceased to exist.

29 What was the result?

The collapse of the mighty capital sent a thrill down through the world and out to the last village on the fringe of civilization. Every little subject kingdom that had groaned under the burden of tribute saw in the crash of Assyrian power the promise of freedom and the hope of better days. There was probably more rejoicing throughout the world than had been known at any time in two hundred years. Among the celebrants there were none in which enthusiasm rose to a higher pitch than among the citizens of Judah. And to the celebration of the fall of Nineveh, in a magnificent and colorful Temple ceremony, we owe another book of the Old Testament—the prophecy of Nahum.

30 Did Judah become independent?

At the time of the fall of Nineveh (612 B.C.) the devout Josiah was still upon the throne. The reforms inaugurated under the authority of the Book of the Law (Deuteronomy 5:26, 28) were at their height. The prophetic party was popular. The collapse of the "harlot" (to use Nahum's designation, 3:4) inspired the hope that Judah might again be free after nearly a century and a half of vassalage. But the fall of Assyria meant no more than a new alignment of old forces, and within three years the little Hebrew state was caught again between the crushing weight of two powerful neighbors locked in a death struggle.

31 What about this new crisis?

When it appeared that Assyria was going down and Babylon was rising to world mastery, Egypt rushed to the assistance of her agelong enemy; but it was too late. The weight of Babylonian arms was too great. Even the help of Egypt was insufficient to save the doomed Empire.

With Assyria finally disposed of Babylon turned on Egypt and, in the battle of Carchemish (605 B.C.) won again. The entire East was immediately open to the attacks and enslavement of the new mistress. For a few years Jehoiakim, king of Judah, paid grudging tribute to the new overlord and then, fired by ambition and badly advised, he revolted. Nebuchadrezzar, the Babylonian king, busy about other matters, was content to loose upon the Judeans the wild desert tribes (II Kings 24:1-2). Life then became stark terror. No one knew when or where the merciless marauders might appear. When Nebuchadrezzar had more pressing problems solved in other parts of his far-flung

17

empire, he turned about and marched upon Jerusalem. In a swift campaign he reduced the kingdom to impotency, took its king captive, and carried off thousands of captives, much booty, and an enormous amount of treasure. Then, having put a puppet on the throne, he retired again to Babylon (II Kings 24:10-17).

32 How long did this last?

The first invasion of Judah occurred in the year 597 B.C. Since the death of Josiah in 608 B.C. the Judeans had been paying their tribute to Egypt, but after the battle of Carchemish (605 B.C.) and the triumph of the Babylonians the annual payments had flowed east instead of south. It was the tax burden which caused the revolt referred to in Question No. 31, and which led to the invasion.

It is highly probable that Nebuchadrezzar had no intention of destroying Jerusalem. All he wanted was some local ruler who would collect the tribute and remit it promptly. At any rate he did not interfere with the government of Judah in any way except to carry off the king (Jehoiachin), who had reigned only three months, and put in his place a son of Josiah whom he named Zedekiah (II Kings 24:11-17). But a radical group of politicians gathered about the new king (Jeremiah 24) who became very arrogant (Ezekiel 11:15) and bold. In an almost incredible spasm of conceit they persuaded Zedekiah to renounce his allegiance to Babylon (586 B.C.), even though there was not the slightest chance for success. This time the whole power of Babylon was loosed upon the Judeans. Their capital, Jerusalem, was completely destroyed, and thousands more of her most energetic and useful citizens were carried away into captivity. In this disaster the long and tortured history of the little Hebrew kingdom came to a pitiful and unnecessary end.

33 Was the city completely destroyed?

The walls were breached, the Temple was razed to the ground, and the entire city was reduced to a pile of rubble. It could almost have been said that there was not left "one stone upon another." The best of the people—artisans, craftsmen, nobles, merchants, the learned, priests, prophets—were all carried away to Babylon as captives. Only poor peasants were left to occupy the land (II Kings 25:4-12). It was a characteristic piece of oriental brutality, executed with callous efficiency and merciless thoroughness. But we have at least one beautiful fragment, bequeathed to us from the times—the book of Lamentations, which consists of a series of poems produced by some prophet-poet who suffered and agonized through those terrible days and who wrote of what he saw in lines of exquisite pathos and awful beauty.

34 Did any prophets preach during these last days?

Perhaps the greatest of them all! Through those last terrible experiences the voice of God was heard among the people, exhorting, warning, challenging, rebuking, advising. Because of the staggering problems with which he dealt, and the positive genius he displayed for original religious thought, there are those who would rate Jeremiah, the prophet of the deathdays, as the greatest Hebrew who lived between Moses and Jesus.

35 What can we say of this period of Hebrew history?

From a political standpoint it was the most disastrous that could be imagined. With Israel destroyed by the Assyrians the entire hope of any future rested with Judah. Her natural situation was advantageous, and, except for bad management on the part of her politicians, she might have continued in something resembling independence through many years; but her short-sighted leaders and the impatience of her people, under burdens that were admittedly heavy, led her to complete destruction.

From a religious standpoint, however, the century was far from being a failure. With an amazing devotion to duty and to the ideals bequeathed to them by Isaiah, throughout the dark days of Manasseh's half century of reaction the little band of unknown and unnamed disciples designated by history as the "prophetic party" kept the fires of Yahwehism burning in spite of persecutions, reverses, political disasters, and popular indifference. Then, through awful days of rioting, bloodshed, and civil strife, ending finally in invasion and destruction, they held the torch aloft and actually passed the light of faith on to their children brighter than it had ever been in all the generations before. Though the political fortunes of the nations

19

were in total eclipse when the period came to a close, the light of personal and individual religion was shining like a beacon to guide the bewildered people.

This dreadful century, in spite of the political collapse with which it closed, and the apostasy which characterized many of its decades, produced four prophets whose writings found their way into the Bible, a book of law which became *the first book of recognized scripture and, ultimately, the core of the Bible,* and a collection of poems called "Lamentations."

True, the writings of the prophets Zephaniah and Nahum do not reach to great spiritual heights, but they reflect the efforts of deeply religious minds as they struggle with cataclysmic political events. On the other hand the sermons of Habakkuk, and especially of Jeremiah, are priceless treasures by the assistance of which confused men through the centuries have found their way across the rubble and wreckage of civilizations into the presence of God. Produced in the midst of hysteria and panic, they have demonstrated their worth most fully in hours of crisis.

36 Who was Zephaniah?

Unlike most of the prophets, Zephaniah goes to great pains to identify himself. In the very first verse of his book (1:1) he traces his ancestry back to Hezekiah. While he does not specify that his great-great-grandfather was King Hezekiah, the majority of scholars believe that to have been the case; and if they are correct in that belief the young prophet was an aristocrat, born to honor and probably to wealth, whose home was in Jerusalem (1:4). We know he was a close observer of the political scene (1:10; 11) during one of the most terrifying periods of Hebrew history.

37 When did he prophesy?

It is impossible to fix an exact date, but we know that he preached while the whole Palestinian world was cringing in terror before the prospect of the Scythian invasion (630-625 B.C.).

38 Why were the Scythians so feared?

(See also Question No. 18.) For twenty-eight years these barbarians drove down from the steppes north of the Black Sea,

20

sweeping across the earth like some dreadful scourge. They built no cities, established no civilization, and organized no government, but lived only for plunder and left every land desolate upon which their feet rested. Like packs of wolves coming out of the woods they raided the lands of the East, and no man was safe except when behind thick walls and heavily barred gates. For five fearful years the little kingdom of Judah lived on the border of panic. Much of our information concerning the Scythians comes from the historian Herodotus, concerning whose accuracy there is some question at this point, but the general condition can be recognized rather well. The people watched the uncouth and savage swarms raging down the caravan routes and up to the very gates of Egypt, where they were bought off by a huge bribe. Then, cowering in abject terror, they saw them return by way of Ashkelon to plunder the beautiful Temple of Aphrodite. Their foul hands ruined that which they could not build, and destroyed a store of treasures they could not create. While all the world of the East held its breath in momentary expectation of death, the agonized cry of Zephaniah was heard above the awful silence.

39 Was Zephaniah a professional prophet?

He was in no way connected with any professionally religious group. He may have been a member of the prophetic party, but of that we cannot be sure. He seems to have been a man of moral insight, sensitiveness, and culture. He can best be described as a layman whose religious integrity was shocked by the general immorality of the nation, and who was convinced that the end of civilization was at hand because of the wickedness of the world, and especially because of the faithlessness of Judah.

40 Why call him a layman?

Because he had no official connection with the religious establishment of his day, so far as we know. Like Amos, he was compelled to speak by the force of the circumstances in the midst of which he lived, and he asked for no more respectful hearing than the worth of his words required. But it was unusual, to say the least, that an aristocratic youth with such connections as Zephaniah had—a member of the "right-wing group" in Jerusalem—should be found among the caustic critics

21

of the government, declaring that the nation's tragedy was caused by social and economic sins.

41 What was wrong with the government?

The nation was ruled by a boy king, Josiah, only seventeen years of age, who was just beginning to assert his own mind. A half century of paganism, government-sponsored, with all its attendant immorality and economic oppression, was only one short decade in the past. In spite of the fact that the farmers and landowners from the rural districts had put Josiah on the throne, the political ring in Jerusalem was not broken up. Nobles, princes, and courts were corrupt, and integrity and honor among the people was at low ebb. So far as the future was concerned it seemed at the moment that the world would have lost little if the kingdom of Judah had been blotted out. Against all this Zephaniah raised his voice in a wild shriek of warning.

42 Was Zephaniah a political prophet?

He could not be anything else. He lived and preached in a time when the world seemed to be shaking to pieces, and when it appeared that everything sacred and precious was going into the discard. Frantic men were asking frenzied questions. It was impossible to withdraw into some safe retreat, there to meditate on the great mysteries of life and philosophy. Men had no time for abstract themes. The few virile and honest minds of the nation were wrestling with the whole question of human destiny and of the security of civilization. It is evident that Zephaniah approached the question from the standpoint of religious faith; but it was impossible to leave the problem of politics and public morals alone, just as it was impossible to ignore the sufferings of the people.

43 What launched his career as a prophet?

Isaiah saw the Lord "high and lifted up" in the Temple and was moved by the vision to begin preaching to the nation (Isaiah 6:1-13). Hosea passed through a bitter domestic experience which awakened him to an understanding of the love of God (Hosea 2:1-5). Amos was impressed by the symbolism of a series of visions (Amos 7:1-2; 8:1-2; 9:1). But Zephaniah records nothing which explains his "call" in any way. Aside from the fact that he began preaching in the midst of a terrible crisis, and that his messages reveal the hot heart and the sensitive spirit of a man who is devoted to Yahweh, we know nothing of the spiritual experience through which he may have passed in receiving his message. At least he lays no claim to any miraculous circumstances as authority for his words.

44 Was Zephaniah concerned exclusively with the Scythians?

His ministry was devoted entirely to the issues raised by the Scythian crisis. He watched the barbarians scorching the earth and believed that the end of civilization had come. He was sure they were the forerunners of a terrible catastrophe which was to engulf the whole world. Although he used poetry, with some exaggeration, to express his thought, he seemed to think that the awful scourge meant the destruction of everything (Zephaniah 1:2-3).

45 Was the situation really serious?

The political situation was very serious. Even though the Scythians did not actually attack Judah, Zephaniah can be forgiven for thinking that this was a part of their plan; for if they had turned their malevolent eyes on the little nation it would have had little hope of surviving.

46 What was the cause of the trouble?

According to Zephaniah the whole disaster was chargeable to the sins of the nation. The life of the people was saturated with paganism. Heathen rituals, introduced by Manasseh, were performed from the housetops of Judah with the sun, moon, and stars receiving homage. The priests themselves were profane, swearing by the pagan divinities. Everywhere the Assyrian cults flourished openly (1:4-6). But to Zephaniah the political disaster was the direct result of the moral and spiritual disintegration which had set in upon the land, and for this he held the princes and leaders (the politicians and capitalists) of Jerusalem directly responsible (1:8-9).

47 With what did he charge them?

He very frankly says that the evils which have done so much

damage originated in the commercial and business life of the capital. The "Fish Gate," the "Second Quarter," and the "Mortar" (business centers corresponding to "Wall Street," the "stockyards," the "stock exchange" in modern life) are mentioned by name. Here the exploitations were planned, the cunning extortions were organized, and the financial manipulations were devised. The young prophet could almost hear the wails coming from these quarters as the guilty plunderers of the people were plundered in turn by the Scythians (1:10-11). For them there was to be no escape; they would be like criminals sought out in the night by armed police who carry lamps. Their homes and their property were to be a forfeit for their paganism (1:12-13).

48 Were only the leaders guilty?

For a hundred years the land had been under Assyrian influence, and it had been impossible to shut the minds of the people against the pagan religion, economics, and social idealism which stemmed from Nineveh. Pagan ways were absorbed by the masses while the manners of the overlord were aped by the fashionable folk of Jersualem (1:8), for this was the easiest way to get along with the masters. The tendency was especially noticeable in the case of Assyrian superstitions.

49 What about Assyrian superstitions?

The Assyrians believed, for instance, that houses were infested with demons which lurked at the thresholds to seize the unwary. The only way to avoid the danger was to leap over them upon entering a house; and all over Judah one might see Hebrews entering their homes thus (1:9). Like the spread of modern astrology, this was an indication of the breakdown of true religious faith; and to Zephaniah it was a symptom of a serious decay in the national life.

50 What did Zephaniah have to say about all this?

Aware of the impending danger from the Scythians, and convinced that Judah had earned her fate by her profligacy and apostasy, Zephaniah pictured the nation as about to be consumed. Yahweh, he said, was like a priest who has prepared a sacrificial meal. The Scythians had been invited to sit down to the meal and consume Judah, and no doctrine of the "day of Yahweh" would save them.

51 What was this doctrine of the "day of Yahweh"?

This was a doctrine that went back many years in Hebrew thought. Amos met it in his day (750 B.C.) and combated it vigorously (Amos 5:18-20). Isaiah, a hundred years before Zephaniah, had also condemned the popular version of the doctrine (Isaiah 22:12-22).

There is a certain similarity between the ancient doctrine of the "day of Yahweh" and the modern doctrine of the second coming of Jesus, as the latter belief is held by some people. To the masses of Judah it meant a day when Yahweh would bare his mighty arm, overthrow all Judah's enemies, and by some tremendous cataclysm establish an entirely new order of affairs, with Judah as the new master of all the world. Every time the national fortunes began to run low this doctrine was put forward by the priests and professional prophets as a means of bolstering up public opinion.

Now the doctrine of the "day of Yahweh" did have a genuine religious significance. It rested back on the idea that Yahweh was the ruler of all the earth and that his moral judgments applied to all peoples; and the great prophets did not combat the fundamental thesis, but the popular misconception of its meaning and purpose.

52 What did Zephaniah think of the doctrine?

The prophet believed that a day of Yahweh was coming, but he believed that it was to be a day of wrath and retribution rather than a day of triumph and vindication. It was to be a day when brutal warriors would overrun the land (Zephaniah 1:14) and terrible calamities would befall the people (1:15). The Scythians were merely the heralds of the day, and when the real blow fell neither the silver for which they had struggled so hard nor the gold for which they had paid such a price would be able to save them (1:18).

53 When did the prophet expect the day to come?

The doctrine had been discussed among the Hebrews for considerably more than a hundred years, and since nothing had happened the people had come to look upon it with a certain good-natured derision. They took much the same attitude as that taken by the early Christians when the second coming of Christ was delayed. But Zephaniah believed the day was approaching with incredible speed (1:14) and was to be accompanied by frightful convulsions of nature (1:15). The bugle blasts and the battle cries of the barbarians were but its heralds (1:16). Even more terrible than the inhumanity of the Scythians was to be the blinding, destroying supernatural forces which Yahweh would let loose upon the world (1:17). Bribes would be of no avail, for the nation would be dealing with Yahweh and not with people (1:18), and Yahweh was not susceptible to bribery.

54 Was Judah to be the only sufferer?

In something of the same mood as Amos, when he discussed the sins of Israel's neighbors (Amos 1 and 2), Zephaniah pictured the whole world as having sinned against Yahweh. The Philistine (called "Cherethites" by the Judeans—see Ezekiel 25:16) cities of Gaza, Ashdod, Ashkelon, and Ekron were all to be destroyed. In time there would be no trace of them (Zephaniah 2:2-7); Egypt (called "Ethiopia") is to perish by the sword; Assyria, the age-long oppressor, was to come tumbling to earth (2:13-14), and her great palaces were to be the haunts of owls, porcupines, and ravens (2:14). Nineveh was to become a refuge for wild beasts, and all men would look on the once-proud city with scorn (2:15).

55 Did the prophet see no hope whatever?

The terrible day he had in mind was still in the future, even though he was perfectly sure it could not be delayed much longer. He saw no reason why it should not fall upon the people, yet he dared to hope they might be saved. If they would honestly seek Jehovah, mend their ways, assume an attitude of humble and genuine penitence, set about to establish justice, turn from oppression, and set their hearts upon him, the doom might yet be forestalled (2:1-3); but the time was short and the nation must make up its mind and act quickly.

56 Did the prophet believe this possible?

Reformation was certainly needed. The rulers of the nation were like ravening lions; the judges of the courts were corrupt; knavery was planned under cover of darkness; the prophets of the day were faithless, declaring only their own imaginings; priests were false to their office; the moral conscience of the entire nation was blurred, and all of this could lead to but one result—*woe* (3:1-4). Jerusalem was still the beloved city of Yahweh; but the people had been warned in the fates that had befallen other rebellious cities (3:5-7), and Jehovah must proceed to carry out his awful purpose, even though he would willingly spare them if a way could be found to do it. (3:8).

57 What basis did he have for this hope?

Even while Zephaniah was thinking of the terrible sins of the nation he was aware of the fact that the great majority of the common people—the humble and the poor—were just, fair, and sincerely desirous of living upright lives. Living quietly upon the land, and of small social importance, they were actually the hope of the nation's salvation. Like Lincoln, Zephaniah believed Yahweh loved the common people upon whom rested the responsibility for carrying forward the nation's hope. There is something of the spirit of Amos and Lincoln in the closing lines of this little book of prophecy (3:11-13). The proud and sinful will be destroyed, but the humble and the righteous will be saved. Somewhere the righteous remnant will be preserved, and from that fraction God will develop his ultimate plan.

58 Was Zephaniah's prophecy fulfilled?

The Philistine cities were sacked and destroyed by the Scythians in much the fashion Zephaniah anticipated. But Nineveh withstood their attacks, though their assaults shook the Empire; and it stood up for more than fifteen years after they retired beyond the northern mountains. Judah did not fall, as the prophet had anticipated, nor was it even so much as besieged. It was at least forty years afterward that it fell to the Babylonians, whose rise to power Zephaniah did not foresee. In this there is a serious word of caution for modern students of prophecy.

59 What is that word of caution?

There is a tendency to think of the prophets as men who predicted the whole course of future events with absolute accuracy. Some teachers of the Bible hold that they were not

27

speaking their own minds, but were little more than recording devices who wrote down the words of God which were given them in some miraculous manner. But if this were true, surely the prophets would have told us, and they do not; furthermore, if the words were proven to be incorrect, then God would be the one making the mistake. The best interpretation therefore is to accept the prophets as righteous and godly people to whom God did make some things plain. But in expressing those things, in explaining those ideas, the prophets were limited by human speech, human understanding, and human events.

60 In what respect was Zephaniah right?

In his condemnation of the immoralities of his time, in his insistence that the nation could not expect the favor of Yahweh if it did not deal justly with its own people, in his repudiation of the pagan cults, and in his assertion that Yahweh was master of the destinies of all nations.

61 What weight did his words carry in Jerusalem?

We have no way of knowing what influence the prophet may have exercised, but it is reasonable to believe that the fact that he was able to speak frankly and critically without being silenced by the government was of great encouragement to the prophetic party, which, through his words, had broken a silence of nearly three quarters of a century. There is a sense in which it may be said that Zephaniah paved the way for the acceptance of the Book of the Law.

62 When was the Book of the Law published?

We have no way of knowing just when it was written, but it came to light in a most dramatic fashion in the year 621 B.C., only a few years after Zephaniah had prophesied and after the Scythian threat had been dissipated.

63 What was the drama in its publication?

The young king Josiah was on the throne in the eighteenth year of his reign (twenty-six years of age) when he decided that the Temple was in need of repairs. The story is told in some detail in Second Kings (chapter 22). The walls were repaired, the floors were put into shape, rotted supporting beams were replaced, and the dilapidated building was generally rehabilitated (II Chronicles 34:1-14). Carpenters, masons, builders, and decorators in large numbers were employed and a considerable sum of money expended.

In the process of repairing the Temple Hilkiah, the high priest, came upon a book which seemed to have some special significance. He called a scribe named Shaphan and asked that the book be read and explained. That worthy man was so deeply impressed that he carried it to Josiah and read it to him, whereupon the king became greatly agitated and gave orders that it should be investigated. It is at this point in the story that a very interesting figure enters the picture.

64 Who was this interesting person?

Her name was Huldah, and she seems to have been a woman of considerable importance in the realm, for the record goes to great pains to identify her (II Kings 22:14; II Chronicles 34:22-28). Her husband, Shallum, enjoyed very intimate relations with the royal court (II Chronicles 34:22) and was something of an artist.

But Huldah had established a reputation in her own right as a prophetess, and very evidently the question of the book was referred to her because her piety and devotion to Yahweh were well known. It is entirely possible that she was one of the prophetic group that was becoming bolder in expressing its views under the encouragement of Josiah's friendliness. Certainly it is extremely interesting that the king should have consulted a *woman* in such a matter, for by that choice *the honor of being the first to declare any religious literature among the Hebrews to be scripture goes to a woman!*

65 How was this done?

It is quite possible that Huldah knew about the existence of the book long before it was submitted to her for judgment. If she had been a member of the prophetic group it is very likely that this was true, but it is impossible to make any such positive statement. At any rate, when she had read it through carefully she solemnly announced that the book contained the law of God and that it was to be obeyed by the nation.

Josiah was so impressed by Huldah's words that, in a royal ceremony to which all the people were bidden, the Book of the

Law was read aloud and declared to be the law of the land. With that it became the written constitution of Judah and the first writing in the Hebrew language to become scripture.

66 Where did the book come from?

There seems to have been a place of safekeeping for the Temple funds, and when the high priest went in to get funds with which to pay the workmen he found the book. No one knows how long it had been there, nor who had secreted it in its hiding place, though credit is given to the prophetic party.

67 What did the prophetic party have to do with it?

Upon the death of Hezekiah, as we have learned, the prophetic party was driven into hiding; and there for almost fifty years it continued in its labors. It is necessary to re-create the situation out of our imagination, for no records remain to us. But faithful men, in spite of martyrdoms and persecutions, kept the fires of faith alive and burning. All about them the nation sank into abysmal depths of licentiousness and healthenism. The most sacred precincts were invaded and despoiled; priests and professional prophets alike were prostituted; protesting voices were silenced in the most effective possible manner— death; the full weight of royal authority was thrown in on the side of the forces of disintegration.

Except for the dogged faithfulness of that little company of unknowns who gathered in secret and furnished one another with courage and hope, Yahwehism most surely would have died out among men. Many took their lives in their hands and defied the dangers of their day in order to affiliate with the prophetic group. Heroic souls braved the threats of death and kept the finy flame burning. Day after day they mused over the inspired writings of their heroes, the great eighth-century writing prophets. They compared those utterances with the facts of their day, studied the ancient laws that had come down under the sacred name of Moses, applied the principles of *mishpat* to the abuses of their time, and reached profound convictions.

Forbidden all other means of expression and in danger of death if they spoke openly, the prophetic party wrote their convictions down. Day by day and month by month, running into the years, these convictions developed and the record grew. Finally, many devout souls having contributed their thought and their godly judgments to the whole, it took form in a code of law and was written into a book. For the first time in Hebrew history there was a system of *written* law.

68 When was the book written?

Generally speaking there was a remarkable degree of free speech among the Hebrews. In no other nation of the ancient world could Elijah, for instance, have rebuked a king and escaped with his life. Micah and Isaiah would have been executed without a trial. The single notable exception to this rule was the period covered by Manasseh's reign (696-642 B.C.), when an absolute silence was imposed upon the prophets. It seems quite reasonable to believe that the book was written sometime toward the close of Manasseh's repressive reign, for if it had been a product of Josiah's time there would have been no reason for secretiveness. By the year 650 B.C Manasseh had reigned for forty-six years, and everyone knew he could not last much longer. It seems reasonable then to think it was hidden away in the Temple about that time.

69 How could that be done?

The royal approval of paganism had seen the Temple of Yahweh neglected. Its services were shared with the ceremonies at the pagan shrines. The fact that Josiah found the building in a sorry state of repair indicates that it was given only scant attention. It is easy then to imagine some aged members of the prophetic party concealing it under their robes and, during some visit to the Temple, finding a way to hide it away in the safe where the records were kept.

70 Who wrote the book?

When the book was submitted to Huldah she merely said that it contained the words of God. But the nation attached the name of Moses to the work, and throughout the rest of its history it has been called the law of Moses.

As the original source and author of Hebrew law, Moses was a tradition, a venerated hero, a spiritual godfather, and the religious mentor of the race. Anything that could claim the authority of Moses was certain to receive a respectful hearing at the hands of the people. The prophetic party, in their secret councils, had made the most earnest effort to interpret the mind of Moses in the light of the conditions under which they lived six hundred years after Moses had been gathered to his fathers.

The laws of Moses had been given in the desert, and the prophetic party was living in a fruitful land under entirely different circumstances. The original code had been prepared for a people who were living a nomadic life, without any pressing political or economic problems; but the prophetic party was confronted by a world in which politics, economics, theology, and national security were inextricably mixed. It was something as if John Wesley, in a day when there were no telephones, motor cars, world-wide economic systems, or global wars, had written a code for the government of the lives of the people called Methodists. To be true to the spirit of Mr. Wesley it would be necessary for the Methodists to bring the application of his principles up to date in each generation. In the case of the prophetic party, it was simply attempting to bring the principles of Moses up to date and into contact with the new set of problems.

When the prophetic party declared that the code they offered was the "law of Moses," they did not attempt to deceive the people into thinking that Moses had actually written the exact manuscript they were submitting. They were probably satisfied to have the people adopt their code as an application of the principles of Moses to the problems of their time. Certainly its temper and purpose were Mosaic. It was a common practice of the day to put speeches made in the spirit of great characters upon their lips, and to credit them with the authorship. The fact that the king and people of Judah accepted the Book of the Law as being *representative of the spirit of Moses* indicates that the prophetic party had done their work well. If there had been any serious contradiction their book would have been repudiated.

71 How did the book proceed?

It followed four great principles, each of which was amplified by a series of special provisions.

72 What was the first principle?

The book took the position that no loyal Hebrew could have anything to do with the worship of any pagan god. Yahweh alone was to be worshiped, and all foreign gods and foreign worship were to be outlawed (Deuteronomy 5:7 ff.; 12:29—13:18).

73 What was the second principle?

The fact that Jerusalem had been spared the destruction with which the Assyrians had laid waste the rest of Judah in 701 B.C. convinced the prophetic party that Yahweh had a special affection for the city, that it was his sanctuary (Deuteronomy 12:5), and that any other spot where people worshiped was not blessed. The "high places" were regarded as sources of spiritual and moral infection from which disaster was certain to flow out over the land, and for that reason must be destroyed (Micah 5:13; Deuteronomy 12:2-28).

74 What was the third principle?

The licentious rites practiced at the shrines, and the ceremonies in use at the Temple in Jerusalem, were utterly abominable to the prophets. They therefore attempted to purge the Temple worship of its pagan elements and restore it to a moral and ethical base.

75 What was the fourth principle?

Committed as they were to the social and ethical ideals of the writing prophets, they laid down a system of laws which they believed would produce justice for all concerned. We will do well to make comparisons between some declarations of the prophets and provisions in Deuteronomy which carry out those ideals. (Compare Amos 5:10, 12; 8:4, 6; Isaiah 1:17; 10:1-2; and Micah 3:1-3, 11 with Deuteronomy 15:7-8, 11; 16:11, 18; 24:19-22. Compare Isaiah 30:1-5; 31:1-3 with Deuteronomy 17:16. Compare Micah 3:5-8 with Deuteronomy 18:18. Compare Amos 2:8a with Deuteronomy 24:11-13, 18. Compare Hosea 8:4b-6 and 10:5-6 with Deuteronomy 5:8-9.) It will be seen from this that the prophetic urge and passion permeates the entire Book of the Law.

76 What laws did the book contain?

It is impossible to give more than a skeleton outline in the limited space we have, but the student will find it extremely profitable to study the following outline with a good commentary. Study the effort that is being made to provide for justice in each instance.

1. Religious laws: Deuteronomy 12:2—16:17.
2. Officials and their duties: 16:18—18:22.
3. Court processes: 19.
4. Military laws: 20.
5. Domestic regulations: 21:10-21.
6. Humane laws: 21:22—21:12.
7. Sex chastity: 22:13-30.
8. Ritualistic laws: 23:9—24:9.
9. Legal justice: 24:10—25:4.
10. Miscellaneous: 25:5-19.

77 Was the Book of the Law made effective?

Josiah, the king, ordered that its provisions should become the law of the land. In this he was doubtless motivated by two great purposes: (1) He was personally devout, and the thought of restoring Judah to her ancestral faith was very attractive to him. (2) In several sections of the East there was a rising tide of nationalism, in which the little nations as well as some big ones (Egypt) were attempting to revive the interest of the people in their own native culture, race, and religion. Perhaps partly as an expression of this increasing nationalism the beginning was made on the books of Kings.

As for the effectiveness of the Deuteronomic laws, it will be necessary to postpone our inquiry until we make a detailed study of Jeremiah, when the facts will become very evident. Suffice it to say at this point that the results were, for the most part, far from satisfactory.

78 What about the books of Kings?

It was the fixed belief of the prophetic party in Josiah's day that Judah's first duty was to obey Yahweh in accordance with the solemn agreement entered into at Sinai. All true prophets believed that loyalty to Yahweh was the only way of national salvation, and that disobedience and disloyalty were sure to result in national disaster. Some Hebrew, with a long-range view of history and with the prophetic conviction, set out to

34

write a history of the two little kingdoms for the purpose of proving that principle.

79   How did he proceed?

Some historical works were already in existence which he used as source material. There were, for instance, the Book of the Acts of Solomon (I Kings 11:41), the Book of the Chronicles of the Kings of Israel (I Kings 14:19), and the Book of the Chronicles of the Kings of Judah (I Kings 14:29), which may have been government records or private histories. It is possible that the author had a biography of Isaiah; certainly he had access to a group of stories concerning Elijah and Elisha; and doubtless he used the Temple annals. We get from these references a very direct bit of information as to how our Bible came into its present form. The author of Kings says very frankly that he was a compiler.

The author was undertaking to teach religion rather than history; and the records of the two kingdoms from the time of the building of the Temple down to the time of Josiah's reforms were scanned for evidence of the truth of the prophetic theory. Every king was measured by two standards: (1) Was he loyal to Yahweh? (2) Did he support Jerusalem as the one sanctuary whereat Yahweh was to be worshiped? If he met these two tests he was called good; but if not it was said of him that he did "what was evil in the sight of the Lord."

Keeping in mind the fact that he is attempting to write a philosophy of history rather than history itself we find the record much more understandable. At times he gets his dates mixed and at other times he leaves out important historical facts because they do not contribute to his thesis. At still other times he exaggerates to make out his case (as when he says a certain king followed "in the way of Jeroboam" though he ruled only seven days—I Kings 16:19).

80   What was the real purpose of the book?

It was very evidently intended to persuade the people and the government to be loyal to Yahweh and keep his laws. It may even have been written to support the Book of the Law and secure for it popular endorsement. But his principal thesis—safety for the nation lay in obedience to Yahweh—is perfectly plain throughout the work.

81 Was the book completed at this time?

As we shall discover in a later study in this series, some great historians and religionists, many years afterward, gathered up all the important historical books and prophetic writings of the Hebrews and assembled them in a noble body of literature which became the scripture of the nation. In combining the various books and documents it became necessary to edit them, making additions here and there to complete them. Thus it came about that the books of Deuteronomy and First and Second Kings were given some additional material, and of that we shall learn later, Meanwhile we must inquire concerning Nahum.

82 Who was Nahum?

Very little is known of the prophet save that he came from a village called Elkosh, a settlement in southwestern Judah, close to the Philistine and Egyptian borders. At the time he wrote his book, however, he was a resident of Jerusalem.

83 When did he write?

It is comparatively easy to fix the date of his writing because it deals with the destruction of the city of Nineveh, capital of Assyria, which occurred in 612 B.C.

84 What did Nahum have to do with Nineveh?

He was a young prophet connected with the Temple in Jerusalem at the time of Nineveh's fall, and he seems to have been commissioned by the Temple authorities to write a pageant, or liturgical service, to be used in connection with the New Year's festival, when the fall of the oppressor would be celebrated.

85 Is the book of Nahum a pageant?

A careful study of the book by scholars who are familiar with the peculiarities of the Hebrew language and the form of the ancient Temple services has led many to believe that we have in Nahum's book the speeches, solos, choruses, recitatives, and responses of a great Temple spectacle which must have combined music, action, and drama.

86 Why was Nahum connected with the Temple?

It was the year 612 B.C., and Josiah, the devout king, was on the throne. The prophetic reforms, launched in 621 B.C., were under full swing, and the prophets were in the ascendancy. It will be remembered that the glorification of the Temple and its services was one of the major interests of the prophetic party. Therefore the presence of prophets in the councils and administration of Temple affairs was to be expected.

87 What were Nahum's duties?

The prophets were probably the preachers who addressed the people on special occasions, who planned the public services of worship, who wrote hymns and festal songs, and otherwise directed the liturgy.

88 What did the fall of Nineveh mean to Judah?

Utterly ruthless, altogether without mercy, greedy beyond description, the Assyrian Empire during more than one hundred years had sucked the Palestinian states dry. Under the pretense of providing "protection" for her subjects she had drained every land she had ruled, leaving the people economically destitute. She cared nothing for justice and may not have known the word. She made no pretense of spreading culture, but ruled for loot without apology. Nahum used the most revolting word in human speech to describe her—"the harlot. . . . who betrays" (3.4). For the little kingdom of Judah—ravaged, despoiled, impoverished—the overthrow of Nineveh meant freedom, hope, and even life. The day the news of her collapse reached Jerusalem was the happiest the city had known in a hundred years.

89 How did the fall of Nineveh come about?

It is the old story of overexpansion, extended lines, top-heavy administration, restlessness under unjustice, the revolt of the enslaved, and the corruption that attends undisciplined power—a story that has been told on the pages of history concerning a long list of states. But the turning point in Assyria's career came in Egypt.

37

The ancient city Thebes (called "No" or "No-Amon" by the Judeans in honor of the Egyptian god Amon—Jeremiah 46:25; Ezekiel 30:15; Nahum 3:8) was the richest and most magnificent metropolis in the ancient Eastern world. There the treasures of Egypt were piled up—silver, gold, precious stones, brilliantly dyed linen, jewels, great monuments. In the year 661 B.C. the Assyrians sacked the city, carrying off long caravans loaded with fabulously rich spoils. Isaiah had predicted the subjugation of Egypt (Isaiah 19:1-4, 21-25; 31:1), but when the blow fell it sent tremors throughout the ancient world.

The puppets put in power by the Assyrians began to connive and intrigue. Incipient revolts started to develop in various sections of the Empire, the most important and the most dangerous appearing down near the Persian Gulf among the Chaldeans. In 625 B.C. Nabopolassar, at the head of the Babylonians and Chaldeans, defied his overlord and began laying the foundations of a new empire. About the same time, far away to the northeast, the Medes, led by an exceptionally able king, Cyaxares, laid siege to the city of Nineveh and might have overpowered it but for the sudden appearance of the savage Scythians, who came down from the northern slopes of the Caucasus Mountains, forcing them to retire. By the time the Scythian horror had passed, the Assyrian Empire was so weakened by its widespread revolts that even a weak little state like Judah was able to throw off the yoke and for a few brief years under Josiah enjoy the nearest resemblance to independence that the state had known in almost one hundred and fifty years. Then came the final blow.

91 What was the final act in the Assyrian drama?

In the year 616 B.C. three great powers faced one another across the world—Assyria, Egypt, and Chaldea. Assyria, exhausted and spent, was in no condition to defend herself. Chaldea, strong and confident, was eager for the kill. Egypt, smarting under Assyrian domination, feared the power of Chaldean arms as much as the Assyrian tyranny, and knew her chance for freedom lay in keeping Assyria just strong enough to hold Chaldea at bay and yet weak enough that she could not again establish her world mastery.

In 616 Chaldea was about to strike the final blow, and Egypt rushed to the defense of her ancient enemy. At this identical moment the Medes struck again. For a time the scene was confused, and then the Chaldeans and Medes formed an alliance and laid siege to the mighty capital. From June until August the Assyrians held out. But at last the walls were breached; the battered Assyrian army deserted; the Egyptian allies were crushed; the inhabitants of Nineveh were slaughtered; the king fled for safety; and the city was turned into a heap of ruins. Remnants of the mighty military machine continued a scattered and futile resistance for a time, but all the world knew the Empire had ceased to be.

92 Why did Nahum write of Nineveh's fall?

Three great feasts were celebrated each year among the Hebrews. The spring festival was called the Passover, the summer celebration the Feast of Weeks, and the autumn festivities the Feast of Booths. The climax of the last was New Year's, on which day it was the custom to celebrate the enthronement of Yahweh as the God of Judah.

The fall of Nineveh coming late in August, the New Year's celebration of 612 B.C. was to follow a few weeks afterward. Under any ordinary circumstances it would have been an occasion of hilarity and rejoicing because it marked the completion of harvest and the gathering of the year's crops. It included something of the element of our modern Thanksgiving observance. But in 612 B.C., in addition to any joy the people may have had because of abundant crops, there was hilarious joy over the prospect of freedom from the Assyrian yoke. The crowds that came up from all parts of the land to Jerusalem for the feast could be depended upon to develop a delirium of happiness. To capitalize upon this occasion, and to stimulate the nationalistic spirit, Nahum wrote his Temple service.

93 Why was Nahum chosen to write the service?

We have no way of answering this question, for the author gives no hint. But an analysis of his little book reveals him as a man of great religious faith and a poet of extraordinary ability. The permanent values of his little book rest back on his interpretation of the fall of Nineveh as an evidence of God's administration of the world.

94 What was Nahum's interpretation of Nineveh's fall?

Assyria had long been the moral mistress of the world, imposing her cruel and callous demands upon all people. Fire and the sword had been her weapons and slavery and destitution had been the lot of the conquered. In her, wickedness seemed to be in complete possession of the world.

In destroying the "harlot" of the nations God had vindicated his right to expect honor and worship. It was much easier to believe in Yahweh with Assyria lying in the dust. The poet-prophet in his Temple service undertook to portray the fall of Assyria as the great triumph for God.

95 Was Nahum's service actually used?

There is small reason to doubt that it was. Indeed, that may be the reason why it was preserved for us. So great was the joy of the nation, and so significant the event commemorated, that it would have been reasonable to expect the Temple authorities to preserve it. Just who was responsible for its care no one knows, but it is sufficient to say that in the book of Nahum we have all of an ancient Temple service that can be put down in black and white.

96 How does the pageant open?

Just as the New Year's service had always opened with a majestic recital of Yahweh's work of creation, Nahum opened his service with a hymn of praise (1:1-8) in the form of an acrostic poem, which was a familiar literary device among the Hebrews.

97 What is an acrostic poem?

Hebrew poetry, unlike English poetry, does not attempt rhymes. Instead, the lines maintain a certain meter or rhythm. In translating Hebrew poetry into English, much of this form is lost; and readers of the King James Version do not recognize the poetry, for there is nothing in the English to identify it. Fortunately the Revised Standard Version and other recent translations show the poetic lines.

An acrostic poem, a popular form among the Hebrews, was one in which the first letter of each line was the succeeding letter of the alphabet. Sometimes two lines of poetry were used to express parallel meanings, in which case the first word of the couplet was chosen for its index letter. In the 119th Psalm we have an acrostic poem in which the opening word of each stanza was chosen for its index letter. Nahum's hymn was an acrostic poem which used the first half of the Hebrew alphabet, but this of course does not appear in an English translation.

98 Who sang the hymn?

The opening hymn was sung by the great throng of worshipers paying their tribute to Yahweh, the God of vengeance, who reveals himself in a terrible storm as he comes forth to heap judgment upon his enemies. Read the first eight verses of the little book and try to imagine them being sung to some wild chant by twenty thousand voices.

99 What does the hymn mean?

It opens with a portrayal of Yahweh as a terrible God of strength and judgment, so terrible that all nature trembles. In the presence of Yahweh, the sea dries up and growing things wither; all the earth stands in awe. (1:1-5). Nineveh has gone down under the wrath of Yahweh (1:6). There are those among the people of Judah who have never lost their faith and these praise Yahweh (1:7-8).

100 What comes next?

At this point the hymn is interrupted by a question addressed to the people by the priests (1:9a), asking why they are praising Yahweh so lustily. The people answer antiphonally (1:9b-10), saying that it is because God has heaped destruction upon their enemy Nineveh. This prepares the way for the prophet's speech.

101 Who is the prophet who speaks?

It was, in all probability, a brief oration delivered by Nahum himself, in which he declares that his message is direct from Yahweh and is a pledge of deliverance and protection. Upon Nineveh and Nineveh's king dire words of doom are heaped (1:12-14). At this point we may have a song of triumph sung by the prophet, or it may be a continuation of the oration. At any rate it recites a picture of the messenger of Yahweh bringing glad tidings to the city concerning the great deliverance. The Judeans are summoned to keep the feast, perform their vows, and offer their gratitude. At least the Hebrew nation's glory is to be restored (2:1-3). Here begins the drama.

102 What about the drama?

The Hebrews made large use of pantomime in illustrating the spoken word. There are those who believe that Nahum's service included a thrilling spectacle which was enacted while the prophet (or some chosen orator) spoke the words. The attacking force gathers for the assault on the city; the chariots are drawn up in place; the cavalry is out in front; the nobles and leaders gather about their standards; the war machines and battering rams are wheeled into place for striking their resounding blows (2:4-5). Then comes a scene worthy of the most spectacular efforts of the moving pictures.

103 What is this thrilling episode?

The gates of the canals of the Tigris are broken. The mighty waters tear down two and a half miles of the city's walls; the city and the royal palace are inundated; and the queen herself is brought forth unceremoniously, followed by terrified servants (2:6-7).

104 What comes next?

The Assyrians suddenly break and flee, leaving vast quantities of loot behind them. The conquerors, gorging themselves, reduce the city to a heap of ruins, and the once-mighty tyrant is stricken with shame (2:8-10).

105 What is the result?

At this point the congregation takes up another hymn, mocking and taunting. "Where is the great Nineveh?" they ask, sarcastically. "Where is the tyrant who once dragged nations to its lair as a lion drags its prey to its den?" (2:11-12.)

106 What is the answer?

The prophet replies in a dramatic address in which he again pronounces a terrible doom on Nineveh. No longer will

Nineveh's barbarities be let loose upon the earth; the judgment of Yahweh is accomplished (2:13).

107 Are the people satisfied?

They take up the theme again, this time in a wild and furious mockery. The nation which has seduced the world is now but a mass of dead bodies. With a certain fierce joy the congregation (or it may be a chorus of priests) describes the terrible fate of the wicked city (3:1-4). At this point Yahweh speaks.

108 How does Yahweh speak?

Throughout the service the prophet presumes to speak for God, declaring his mind and purposes. It is in these speeches that the strength of the book appears. *Nahum believes he knows the mind of God.* How he came into possession of that knowledge he does not indicate. It is sufficient to say that he assumes the right to speak, declaring that he is speaking Jehovah's words. Here is a mighty spiritual assertion—*a man is speaking for God* (3:5-7).

109 Are the people impressed?

The fact that they preserved the little book is some evidence. But we must remember that Nahum's speeches were only a part of the book; the people again have their voice and express their mind.

110 What is their opinion?

In the days of her arrogant might Assyria had sacked the rich Egyptian city of Thebes (No-Amon) and carried quantities of loot away to Nineveh. The terrible fate that has overtaken the "harlot" of the nations is, according to Nahum's hymn for the people, the judgment of God; and with numerous local political references the people sing a taunt song (3:8-11). The fortifications are useless. Just as ripe figs are devoured by the hungry, Nineveh's conquerors are upon her (3:12-13); and toil as she may, her defenses are in vain (3:14-15). Speaking again in the name of God Nahum assures Nineveh that no armies or warriors can save her. The city is doomed (3:15-17). A congregational hymn closes the service.

111 What is the closing hymn?

All the nations of the earth are rejoicing in the fall of the tyrant; and in a death-song lament such as might have marked the funeral of a notable, Nahum closes his message (3:18-19).

112 Is this a very religious book?

The answer to this question depends upon our definition of the word religious. Certainly there is nothing in the book that hints at any aspect of personal religion. It is nothing more than it pretends to be—a great pageant, or liturgical service, in celebration of the fall of the tyrant and Judah's deliverance. That it has all been accomplished by the power of God Nahum makes perfectly plain. This is the burden of his message. Judah owes all her joy and praise to God, for certainly her own arms have had nothing to do with the glad event. The religious aspect of the book appears in Nahum's insistence that Yahweh is the author of the nation's good fortune—that he is the Lord of history, and that all nations are subject to him. But when the best has been said of Nahum's little book it must still be admitted that it is on a much lower level than Habakkuk's writing.

113 Who was Habakkuk?

A prophet who undertook to sustain the faith of the nation through one of the most hopeless periods of Hebrew history.

114 When did Habakkuk do his writing?

There is some debate on this subject. Until recently it was pretty generally agreed that Habakkuk preached against Babylon, about 600 B.C. But since about 1908 the opinion has grown in some quarters that the name Chaldeans (Habakkuk 1:6) was substituted by some accident for the original *Kittim* (meaning Macedonians, or Greeks), in which case the book should be dated somewhere in the fourth century B.C. The argument for this viewpoint is that the denunciations in 2:5-20 correspond better with Alexander the Great than with the Babylonians of the seventh century B.C., and that the entire book would achieve a better unity if it were so dated.

115 What should our conclusion be?

Fortunately, in the case of Habakkuk the question of date is not of great importance. Whether the prophet wrote in the seventh century of the Babylonians, or in the fourth century of

I trust in you,
I say,
"you are
my God."
My life is in
your hands.
Let your face
shine on your servant.
Save me in
your love.

PSALM 31:15-17

PR-30 The Printery House - Conception, Missouri 64433

the Greeks, makes no difference in the spiritual significance of the message of his book.

116 What is that essential message?

It is the old question which has arisen in almost every generation, and which is being asked in varying forms in our own day—*"Why does a good God permit wickedness to flourish?"* And it is the answer that has strengthened the hearts of the anxious in every generation since Habakkuk wrote—*"the righteous shall live by his faith."*

117 What made the problem acute in Habakkuk's day?

The moral situation inside the kingdom was not good. Law and justice were held in contempt; the pagan cults exercised a baleful influence; robbery and violence were everywhere; the wicked imposed upon the righteous, and the sufferers had no recourse (1:2-4). All this Habakkuk presents in one of the most daring passages in the entire Old Testament.

118 Why call it daring?

Against the wickedness of his day the prophet had protested again and again. He had prayed earnestly over the situation, presenting his appeals to Yahweh over and over, but all to no avail. Now, in desperation, he demands that God shall justify himself and explain his rulership of the world. This is a radical departure for a Hebrew prophet who worshiped Yahweh.

Amos, Hosea, Isaiah, Micah, Zephaniah, Nahum—they had all accepted the world as they found it and had undertaken to explain it in the light of their belief concerning God. But Habakkuk was the first Hebrew thinker who ever presumed to question the wisdom or the justice of Yahweh's administration of the world's affairs. Whereas other prophets undertook to explain God's ways, Habakkuk *called upon God to make the explanation.*

119 Was the problem really serious?

Even the most devout Hebrews believed that piety and prosperity went together as cause and effect. If the nation pleased God it might expect favor; if it failed to please God disaster was sure to follow. Up to Habakkuk's time all the great prophets had undertaken to explain that the nation had sinned, and in what respect it had failed to please God. Their messages were concerned principally with the question of how Yahweh's favor could be won, and how the nation might restore itself in God's good graces, reestablishing the "chosen people" status. But with Habakkuk the problem takes on a new phase.

120 What is that new phase?

Habakkuk was well aware of the wickedness of Judah, but he was also keenly sensitive to the wickedness of the world outside of Judah. As he presents his appeal to Yahweh, asking "Why is wickedness allowed to persist?" he is answered by the assurance that God is about to do an amazing thing—God is going to use the enemy as an instrument for punishing the evildoers (1:6-10). But that only confuses the issue in the prophet's mind, for certainly the enemy is more wicked than Judah. Therefore Habakkuk challenges God for the second time. How can God show favor to a wicked nation and still call for the worship of good people? Has the enemy not defied God again and again? What is the logic in using a very wicked nation to punish another nation less wicked (1:13-17)?

121 What was the answer?

Habakkuk describes himself as taking up a position on the watchtower and there awaiting an answer. In just what form the answer was expected he does not tell us—whether he expected a vision, a divine voice, or a vivid impression laid upon his mind. He does not say, but he is confident that Yahweh will make the answer plain.

The prophet is instructed to take tablets and write upon them the contents of the vision he is about to receive, in characters so large that anyone passing by might read them even though he was hurrying. He is not to be impatient, but to wait for Yahweh. But it must be noted that, whereas the vision was from God, the record of the vision is Habakkuk's.

122 What was the message?

It was a very old conviction of the prophets that a day was coming when the forces of evil and the forces of good would be locked in a mortal combat. In that day Yahweh was to emerge triumphant. In his hour of vision Habakkuk became convinced that the awful brutality and ruthlessness of the enemy was but temporary—that the suffering that was being inflicted upon the world was soon to come to an end because the enemy was doomed. The basis for his message of hope to Judah was that there was something eternal in righteousness which evil could not destroy, and that those who were righteous would survive because they had that eternal element within them. Their loyalty and faithfulness to God would ultimately save them (2:4-5). In his message touching this matter Habakkuk has given us one of the most sublime and magnificent declarations in all the utterances of religion.

123 What is that great saying?

"The righteous shall live by his faith." (2:4.)

The great New Testament writer of Hebrews (10:38), in one of his exalted moments, seized upon that text and set it in as a capstone of Christian doctrine, though he used the words in a slightly different meaning from that intended by Habakkuk. The Apostle Paul likewise appropriated the words (Romans 1:17; Galatians 3;11), with still another meaning. Centuries afterward Martin Luther, in his historic conflict with the Roman Catholic Church, made of those words the rallying cry of the Protestant Reformation. But he too, like the author of Hebrews, gave them a slightly different meaning.

124 What was Habakkuk's meaning?

He believed that there was something in righteousness and faithfulness that would survive the years and prove triumphant, whereas wickedness carried the seed of its own destruction within itself. The faithful and righteous might suffer, but they would survive. In their virtue and faith they had something against which all the evil in the world would prove helpless.

125 What was Paul's meaning?

The great Apostle had in mind that trust in God which roots down in an inner conviction actively expressed in personal surrender to God's will.

126 What did Hebrews mean?

The word here used is better translated "faithfulness," which

47

means that patience and perseverance will be sufficient for salvation; and this is considerably different from Paul's concept.

127 What was Luther's meaning?

Martin Luther seemed to go back to the Pauline concept. He took the position that trust in God, through Christ, would be the assurance of salvation from sin and the punishment of hell.

128 Was Habakkuk satisfied?

He seems to have had his confidence re-established sufficiently to pronounce five woes against the enemy. These he is sure constitute the doom of the wicked one and the vindication of Yahweh.

129 What were those five woes?

The terror of the times made it necessary for Habakkuk to veil his language somewhat, but no Judean could possibly have missed his meaning.

1. The enemy's lust for power, likened to the demands of a merciless creditor, was to be avenged. What he had done to the helpless subject nations would, in time, be done to him (Habakkuk 2:6-8).

2. All the pain which the conqueror had inflicted upon the world would, in time, be inflicted in turn upon him. The mighty walls of his capital, built with blood of the slain, cried out for vengenance (2:10-11).

3. The great cities, built by slave labor, and the vast wealth filched from the world, would go up in smoke (2:12-13).

4. God, as the moral master of the world, would compel the enemy to drink from the same bitter cup which Judah had drained (2:15-16).

5. Legendary dragons and monsters would hurry to assist in the destruction of the monster nation (2:17), and the dumb and lifeless idols would prove an empty mockery with no power to assist the doomed nation (2:18-19). What a contrast to the figure of the living God of the Hebrews (2:20)!

130 What was the basis of Habakkuk's faith?

One central fact dominated his thinking—*he believed that Yahweh would be completely victorious in the great climactic struggle between good and evil.* The forces of evil might enjoy temporary victories and brief triumphs, but in the end *they were doomed because they were evil.* This great conviction he did not attempt to prove, but he asserted it with all the powers at his command.

131 How did he prove his case with the people?

He reported to them that he had come by this assurance in a vision. Convinced that the truth had been given to him direct from God, he asked the people to accept it on his word as from their God (3:2). As God had shown faithfulness to others down through the long years of Judah's history, so, Habakkuk believed, he had shown himself to him (3:3-4). As God had conquered primeval monsters in his work of creating the earth (a popular belief of the times), so he would conquer the evils that were ruining life in the prophet's time (3:8-11). As the Egyptians had met their doom at the Red Sea because of their infamies, so the later enemy would meet their master in Yahweh and perish (3:12-15). With a great prayer of faith and confidence he closes his book (3:16-19).

132 How did Nahum and Habakkuk differ?

Nahum was an intense nationalist. He saw no sins among his own people as Habakkuk did, or even as Zephaniah did. He anticipated no punishment for Judah, but exulted in the terrible fate which had befallen Nineveh. Habakkuk, on the other hand, saw Judah's sins and anticipated their punishment. But as a great religious thinker—which Nahum was not—he undertook to sift the evidence and construct a faith that was both logical and enduring. Perhaps an even greater contrast, however, might be drawn between Habakkuk and his immortal contemporary, Jeremiah.

133 Who was Jeremiah?

The last of the great prophets to minister to the Hebrew people during the days of their political independence. His book is the longest prophetical book in the Old Testament. Because of the sublime religious concepts which it contains, and because of the great spiritual advances which Jeremiah charted, he has been called the "greatest figure between Moses and Jesus."

49

134   When did Jeremiah preach?

It is believed that he was born about 645 B.C., which was ten years before the appearance of the Scythians. He saw the barbarian hordes sweep down over the land and knew all about the terror they inspired and the havoc they wrought. In the day in which he lived everything sacred in life was threatened. He heard the news of the fall of Nineveh and watched the rise of the Chaldean Empire from its first defiance of Assyria until its final triumph at Carchemish (605 B.C.). He was a witness to the collapse of the "harlot" of the nations and was a citizen in Judah when the good king Josiah preached his reforms. He saw armies of Chaldea smash through the feeble defense of Jerusalem and sack the sacred city, and he seems to have been present when the boy king of Judah was dragged from his throne and carried in chains, together with his mother, to Babylon. He watched the pillaging of the capital, the deportation of thousands of the nations' best citizens, and the establishment of the new government which was to take orders from Babylon. He preached to a nation that was gasping out its life in agony and in a hopeless struggle, and he attempted to maintain the faith of a people who watched helplessly while everything they had held sacred was destroyed before their eyes. He saw the last trace of the government of Judah wiped out and was himself kidnapped and carried off to Egypt by a band of his own countrymen who were fugitives from justice. Through all this he was commissioned to preach the judgments of God and to hold up the standards of Yahweh, and he performed his work with a patience and courage that was nothing less than sublime in spite of a disposition that was at the same time tender and sensitive.

135   How did he acquit himself?

As we study his writings we shall discover that Jeremiah reached heights of personal religion, moral judgments, and spiritual understanding never before attained by any Old Testament prophet. If Zephaniah and Nahum do not always inspire us with lofty idealism and rich spirituality, and if Habakkuk does not reach a solution of his problem but stops with a great unproved assertion of faith, still the seventh century B.C. is redeemed by the exalted preaching of Jeremiah.

To him, as to no other Old Testament character, we owe the fundamental concepts of personal religion. He is one of the great spiritual giants of all time, and to explore the majestic heights of his mind and spirit with the aid of his book remains to this day one of the sublime experiences of any man's religious quest. Jeremiah was a thinker who, next to Jesus, plumbed life to its depths.

136 Where did Jeremiah preach?

He was a youth from the village of Anathoth, one of the original thirteen cities assigned to the Levites (I Chronicles 6:60), three or four miles northeast of the city of Jerusalem. It was the last village of Judah toward the east, and just beyond it lay forbidding hills; while just a little farther on was the northern end of the Dead Sea. Solomon, at the beginning of his reign, had vented his spite on Abiathar (David's favorite priest), banishing him to Anathoth with a grand flourish in which he pretended great generosity (I Kings 2:26 ff.). The family to which Jeremiah belonged may have been among his descendants (Jeremiah 1:1), for the young prophet names his father, Hilkiah, and tells us that he was a priest. Thus Jeremiah was in marked contrast to his two contemporaries, Zephaniah and Habakkuk, both of whom seem to have been men of the city, and to Nahum, whose ministry occurred in Jerusalem. He was a rural youth, a winsome boy from the country.

Much of his public ministry occurred in Jerusalem, though he did preach also on occasion at Anathoth, and at least once he seems to have made a tour of the villages and towns about Judea, preaching his doctrines and political policies.

137 What do we know about his private life?

No other prophet gives us so many facts concerning his private affairs as does Jeremiah. At times his book is almost biographical. If one is well versed in the political movements of the times it is possible to detect many references to events and circumstances which were definitely political and economic in their significance.

Jeremiah's father, as we have learned, was a priest (1:1). Before the boy's birth he was dedicated by his parents to the service of Yahweh (1:5). As a son of a priest he was naturally destined for the priesthood, but we have no record of him ever having engaged in any priestly functions. However, from his own testimony we may judge that he was reared in a home where religion was a part of the very atmosphere. The responsibilities of his work as a prophet made it difficult for him to maintain a home, and he seems to have felt it to be a part of his call that he should not marry and rear a family (16:1-4). This enforced loneliness of his heart appears in his book in the form of a great wistfulness. A single reference hints that he may have had brother (12:6), but further than that we know nothing of his immediate family circle. From some source he must have come into possession of some wealth, for he gave himself to his ministry without any apparent effort to earn a living and toward the end of his life he had money with which to buy a field that had belonged to his family estate in an earlier day (32:6 ff.).

138 How old was he when he began preaching?

He states very definitely that the word of Yahweh came to him in the thirteenth year of the reign of Josiah (1:2), which was in 627 B.C. If the estimate that he was born in 645 B.C. is correct it would mean that he was eighteen years old when he began his ministry. This may seem an early age; but when we recall that the Hebrew boy was considered to be an adult at twelve, that many marriages were contracted at the age of sixteen, that at least two kings came to the throne before they were ten (Joash at seven—II Chronicles 24:1—and Josiah at eight—II Kings 22:1), and that a third became king at the age of twelve (Manasseh—II Kings 21:1), it does not seem so improbable that Jeremiah became a prophet at the age of eighteen.

The end of his prophetic career is placed at 586 B.C., following the fall of Jerusalem, which means that his prophetic life covered a period of forty years. Into these four decades he crowded as much adventure, suffering, hardship, and tragedy as ever befell any one individual in the Biblical record. Only Paul, the New Testament Apostle, can hope to equal Jeremiah's record for personal hardships. Isaiah, a hundred years earlier, lived a life of ease and comfort in comparison. There is scarcely a chapter in Jeremiah's book what does not echo with suffering. Yet in spite of all his hardships he spoke out bravely for God and gave himself unstintedly to his ministry without a thought for his personal safety. Never once was he guilty of saving himself at the expense of his message.

139 Why should a priest live at Anathoth?

A very large number of priests were attached to the Temple in Jerusalem, and hundreds made their home in the city. But the services expected of them in connection with the Temple were limited and they had much idle time on their hands, which many of them employed in connection with the local shrines. Weeks together they might not be needed to minister at the Temple at all. They were therefore at liberty to serve as ministrants at the local altars. As long as they were available for their Jerusalem duties they were allowed to live where they pleased. This resulted in several colonies of priests developing in communities within a reasonable distance of Jerusalem. As their services with the local shrines often proved very profitable indeed, the priests were provided with very personal reasons for resenting any interference with the operation of the "high places" and neighborhood altars.

Such a community of priests was to be found in the village of Anathoth. The town seems to have reflected this fact in an atmosphere of religion in the midst of which Jeremiah grew to manhood. It could hardly have been called piety, but at least it was such as would have directed the thoughts of a young man toward religious matters. We know that the local shrine of Anathoth was highly respected, and that when an attempt was made to destroy these local altars in the course of the Josiah reforms Jeremiah encountered bitter opposition among his fellow townsmen. They even conspired against his life. But in spite of the fact that the worship of Yahweh may have been sadly corrupted in Anathoth, the boy Jeremiah was reared in an atmosphere calculated to produce a soul sensitive to spiritual matters.

140 What was the occasion for launching his ministry?

The Scythians were ranging back and forth across the East, threatening preaceful villages and terrorizing whole populations, during the years when Jeremiah was a growing boy. The little nation of Judah cowered in fear at the very mention of the barbarians, and no man knew when the kingdom might be the next victim. Zephaniah must have been preaching his terrible forecast of doom as the young prophet approached his twentieth birthday, and this may have impressed him very deeply.

At any rate Jeremiah grew up with the conviction that he would preach in the name of Yahweh (1:5-6). But when the call actually came he was seized with a great fear that his youthfulness would defeat him. On this point he was reassured by Yahweh; and in describing his experience he cited two visions that came to him, probably while he was trying to think the matter through.

141 What was the first vision?

In Palestine the almond tree is first to send out its bloom in the early spring. For that reason it is called the "wakeful tree" by the Hebrews. One day, as the young prophet stood admiring a blooming almond tree, it suddenly dawned upon him that the tree would not be flowering at all if God were not active in the world, and if God were active in the matter of the almond tree then God must surely be active in the affairs of the nation (1:11-12).

142 What was the second vision?

Some time afterward he sat watching a boiling pot, its face being turned toward the south. The steam was pouring out in that direction. In the midst of his meditation he was impressed with the idea that the Scythians from the north were the agents of Yahweh (1:14-15), and as such were being used as the instrument for punishing Judah for her sins.

143 What did Jeremiah do about it?

The blooming almond tree and the driven steam seemed to constitute a message from God to the people, and a sense of destiny settled down upon his soul, impelling him to deliver his message. He was reluctant to assume the responsibility, knowing that he was an untrained speaker and being keenly sensitive on the subject of his youthfulness (1:6). Both these considerations seemed to bar the way, but with each assertion of reluctance he was assured by Jehovah that his deficiencies would be met (1:7-8). Words would be supplied him, he was told—words of criticism and words of constructive import

54

(1:9-10). After much inner struggle he finally came to his decision, and he preached thereafter with passion and power; but the quiver of his sensitive soul can be felt in his book to this day as he describes the struggles through which he was compelled to pass.

144 Did the times seem auspicious?

Jeremiah believed that the sins of Judah had brought the terrible doom down over the hearts of the people. They had been ungrateful toward Yahweh and they had turned aside to worship pagan gods (2:11-13). But even more, they had relied upon the paganism of Egypt and Assyria to save them from their difficulties instead of putting their trust in the righteousness of Yahweh (2:18, 36). These political alliances with the pagan nations were, to Jeremiah, the equivalent of a repudiation of Yahweh. He believed that Yahweh was abundantly able to take care of his own people, and that to seek outside help was a sin that could not be tolerated. Even though we may be inclined to think of Jeremiah as a Puritan, still it must be admitted that moral, political, and religious conditions in Judah were very bad.

145 What were the political conditions?

The Scythian invasion was rapidly reaching its crest. Cities were going up in flames, property was being destroyed; and people were dying all over the Eastern world. The Assyrian Empire was reeling under the blows of the barbarians, unable to give the subject nations any protection, which meant that Judah was left almost defenseless. The state of Chaldea, with Babylon as its capital, was developing power and threatening the overlord from the extreme southern end of the Empire. The Medes were about to attack on the east, and Egypt was intriguing with the small Palestinian states in the hope of stirring up a revolt that would make her own borders safer. Every well-informed person in the world knew that the entire world was in a state of ferment and that no nation's future was secure. *And on the throne of Judah sat a boy* untrained in military tactics, statesmanship, or administration—utterly unprepared for the vast responsibilities resting upon him.

Jerusalem, as the capital, dominated the nation, and its moral standards were the prevailing ones. Soon after Jeremiah answered his call he made a trip to Jerusalem, probably expecting to find a great spiritual inspiration at the Temple and in the life of the capital; but instead he was staggered at the discovery that wickedness prevailed everywhere. Neither rich nor poor, cultured nor oppressed, gave any evidence whatever of moral conscience. The whole life of the nation appeared dissolute to him. Bribery, exploitation, injustice, poverty, ostentation, licentiousness, drunkenness—these were all common sins (5:1-6), working for the breakdown of the nation's spirit.

147 What were the economic conditions?

We have already learned (Question 22) that Josiah came to the throne of Judah as a result of a revolt in which the poor landowners (*am ha'arets*, meaning "people of the land") slaughtered the reactionary politicians of Jerusalem (II Kings 21:24) and set up a "people's government." The need for such a reform is reflected in Zephaniah (3:1-3), when the prophet said of Jerusalem, "Her officials within her are roaring lions; her judges are evening wolves."

The long years of exhausting vassalage to Assyria, together with wars, invasions, and pillaging, had stripped the nation of the greater part of its wealth. The half century of Manasseh's callous rule had seen large numbers of the poor landowners expropriated. The people were desperately poor; commerce was at a standstill; no wealth was coming into the little land from the outside in the form of tariffs and custom duties; and the general insecurity of the politicial situation discouraged any energetic efforts on the part of either farmers or herdsmen, with the result that the entire nation trembled on the verge of destitution and bankruptcy.

148 What were the religious conditions?

Under Manasseh, who died in 642 B.C. (about three years after Jeremiah's birth), the Assyrian religions had invaded Judah and been accepted by large masses of the people. The young king Josiah, only about twenty-two years of age when Jeremiah began preaching, was well-meaning and naturally devout; but he was not yet strong enough nor wise enough to deal effectively with the evils that were rife in the nation's life. Gross abuses appeared in various quarters. The people had no sense of sin (Jeremiah 2:27); the burning of children as sacrifices to heathen gods was widely practiced (7:31); and pagan practices corrupted the worship of Yahweh at the altars of the Temple. Isaiah had taught the people that the city of Jerusalem would never be destroyed for it was the sanctuary of Yahweh. This gave great comfort to the money-lenders and landlords who made their home therein for they felt that their land-grabbing and exploitation had the sanction of religion. It was a contented and a condemned generation.

149 Was anyone doing anything about it?

The "reform government" had cleaned out the courts and appointed new judges and many dispossessed families had been restored to their lands. The priests of the foreign cults were aware of some threat to their position and the prophetic party was becoming a bit bolder; but Hebrew *mishpat* with its emphasis upon social justice for the poor and exploited, was not yet established. In the face of the whole disordered generation the forces of organized religion were absorbed in pettiness and trivialties (19:14–20:6).

150 What was Jeremiah's first move?

Immediately after Jeremiah settled the matter of his call he seems to have set out for Jerusalem. There he proceeded to warn the nation that the armies from the north (Scythians) would soon break in upon Judah like some terrible calamity. In this he shared the thinking of Zephaniah, who was preaching on the same theme. But it seemed perfectly plain to Jeremiah that they were Jehovah's agents, appointed to punish Judah; and with all the earnestness of which he was capable he pleaded with the nation to repent (4:3 ff.), abandon the popular paganism (2:1-13, 20-35) and repudiate all foreign alliances (2:14-19, 37 ff.). If he could move the city he could save the nation.

151 Did he see no hope?

He foresaw terrible suffering and anguish for the people unless there was a change in the nation's policy, together with sincere repentance (4:19-20). In vivid pictures he interpreted the times (4:23-26) and portrayed Jerusalem in the throes of death (4:31). Those must have been awful days for the young prophet, and they could not have been easy for the young king upon the throne who had to assume the responsibility of acting. Jeremiah scanned the heavens for any ray of hope and saw nothing to justify the slightest confidence that even a remnant could be saved (6:27-30). Yet, probably inspired by Isaiah's faith, he persisted in the belief that in some way a remnant, no matter how small and pitiful, would survive and upon that narrow base Yahweh would begin to build again. The foolishness of the people, and their stubborn refusal to follow in the way of Yahweh, moved him to hot indignation (6:11-14). Again and again he called attention to the advances of the barbarians (5:6, 15-17; 6:1-8, 22-28, 8:14-17). The prospect filled his soul with agony (8:18—9:1, 10 ff., 17-19, 20-22).

152 How was Jeremiah's message received?

No prophet of doom is ever popular, and Jeremiah was no exception. But the young prophet of Anathoth faced at least two conditions which made his work extremely difficult.

As has been mentioned, Isaiah preached the doctrine of Jerusalem's inviolability. It was a special message for a special time, serving its purpose well at the time it was first preached. The Assyrians were just outside the walls; Hezekiah the king was in terror; and Isaiah was sure that God had promised the safety of the city. When the city was delivered, and the Assyrians were in full retreat, Isaiah found himself highly esteemed as a preacher and political interpreter. But during the hundred years that followed the deliverance of Jerusalem Isaiah's doctrine of inviolability was expanded into a dangerous doctrine, as often happens with a doctrine of miracle. The people had been taught that nothing could even happen to the capital, no matter how wicked or unworthy it might become; and the result was that the doctrine which was orignally intended to comfort a stricken people became an opiate for a people engrossed in practicing injustices. Jeremiah's predictions of the city's fall were regarded as rank heresy by such a generation, much as some people regard that one as a heretic who questions the doctrine of the second coming of Jesus.

But even more than his denial of the doctrine, Jeremiah was the victim of a strange belief concerning the prophets themselves. The people had been taught a doctrine—perhaps by self-seeking prophets who terrorized them—that any man who spoke for God had the power to bring his own words to pass. The belief resembled, in some small degree, the belief in witchcraft. At any rate, as Jeremiah preached the doom of Judah and Jerusalem the people believed that his very words were working to bring about the destruction he forecast. This made him their actual enemy, and he was considered both a heretic and a destroyer. This misunderstanding of his purpose, and the bitter opposition of the people, constituted a great grief for the prophet (15:10; 20:7 ff.), who sought nothing but the nation's good and saw clearer than anyone else the devastating effect of sin.

153 Did history vindicate Jeremiah?

The Scythian invasion did not result in any such dire calamity as Jeremiah expected. Jerusalem was never even attacked, and aside from some small plundering raids on border villages, Judah does not seem to have suffered. Certainly the prophet's words were never fulfilled, and his worst fears were never realized.

154 What was the effect upon Jeremiah?

In the eyes of his contemporaries he was branded as a false prophet whose sermons were mere harangues. His predictions concerning the Scythians having failed, the people could scarcely be blamed for doubting the rest of his preaching.

But more serious than the reception given to his sermons by the public was the effect of his mistaken preaching upon his own spirit. He seems to have been badly shaken in his own mind. For a considerable period following the collapse of the Scythian threat he maintained a discreet silence. This may explain a rather interesting question.

155 What is that interesting question needing explanation?

The most important religious event of Jeremiah's lifetime, and one of the most important in all the Old Testament, was the finding of the Book of the Law in 621 B.C. It will be remembered that this book was submitted to *a prophetess* for judgment. In view of the fact that Nahum, Zephaniah, and Jeremiah were all active at this time, and certainly Jeremiah must have been well known, it seems strange that none of them should have been consulted in a matter so important. Zephaniah was of the royal house; Nahum was a part of the Temple organization; and Jeremiah was a conspicuous preacher. These are those who explain the choice of Huldah on the grounds that Jeremiah had been discredited by the failure of his predictions concerning the Scythians. And concerning another important question there is a considerable mystery.

156 What is the second mystery?

In the year 612 B.C. the mighty city of Nineveh fell, and in that event the mastery of the world changed hands. Here was an occurrence of very great significance, but it is extremely difficult to prove that Jeremiah actually said anything about it. Some passages from his book might indicate that he had the stricken capital in mind, but the references are sufficiently vague to allow for considerable questioning. One can hardly think of Jeremiah remaining silent under such circumstances, however, unless he had been terribly shaken in his own confidence. There remains, however, one more mystery.

157 What is that third mystery?

It is impossible to know just when the Book of the Law was composed, though knowledge that it was in existence must have been more or less common among the members of the prophetic party. This is supported by the manner in which Huldah, a member of the party, passed such glib judgment upon it. Yet there is no indication that Jeremiah had any knowledge of the book or that he shared any of the confidences of the members of the party in regard to it. When its reforms were launched, however, he threw himself heartily into the effort to make them effective.

158 What was the effect of the Scythian invasion?

There can be no doubt that the nation was thoroughly frightened by the prospect of destruction, and to this doubtless

60

Zephaniah and Jeremiah contributed largely. But when the danger was past many probably said, "We were not really worried." Yet the threat did unquestionably prepare the way for Josiah's reforms.

159 What were those reforms?

Again we must be reminded that Josiah was put into office by a people's movement, and for a considerable number of years the king's reforms consisted of efforts to correct land abuses. But the discovery of the Book of the Law inspired him to initiate reforms that went down into the very depths of the religious life of the nation. Such was the effort to centralize all worship in the Temple at Jerusalem, the destruction of the rural "high places," the establishment of *mishpat*, and the general suppression of Baal worship (II Kings 23). But the strange fact is that the adoption of the Book of the Law as the official constitution of the land eventually sounded the death knell of prophecy.

160 How did the book put an end to prophecy?

With final authority vested in the written page, and made effective by the doctrine of inspiration, men came more and more to view the spoken word with suspicion. If God had given the inspired *written* word, what use was there for the inspired *spoken* word? As reverence for the written law grew, confidence in the inspiration of the spoken word declined, until finally it was believed that the spirit of prophecy had disappeared from among the people and all authority was ascribed to "The Law." A great forward step was taken in this direction in Ezra's time (400 B.C.), when an enlarged "Book of the Law" was officially recognized; and in Jesus' day the Jews at Jerusalem believed that all inspiration among the prophets had ceased with Ezra.

161 What about the land reforms?

We get numerous hints of these in the references to the land question in Deuteronomy. In Exodus (20:4-17) there is one version of the Ten Commandments and in Deuteronomy (5:7-21) there is another. Scholars are pretty well agreed that the Exodus version is the earlier. This becomes more significant when we notice, for instance, that Deuteronomy says, "And you shall not desire your neighbor's house, *his field*, . . ."

whereas Exodus makes no mention of the field. This suggests that the land question has become acute. Isaiah lashed out against those who coveted the fields (Isaiah 5:8); and Micah, about the same time, said, "They covet fields, and seize them" (2:2). There is a direct reference to the foreclosure proceedings, by which the poor had been losing their lands, in the law against removing the ancient landmarks (Deuteronomy 19:14; 27:17), a process which was a part of the system which had seen the big estates grow up.

The prophetic party made one bold attempt to solve the land question by an enactment which must have seemed pretty radical to the moneylenders of that time, and would certainly seem so to the man with money to invest today. Land loans were to be made without charging interest; and if, at the end of seven years, the borrower had not been able to repay, the lender was to cancel the obligation (Deuteronomy 15:1-2; 23:19-20). This must have seemed a good deal like Communism to those ancient Judean bankers.

162   What about the religious reforms?

The rural "high places" were destroyed and all the religious life of the people was centralized in Jerusalem, leaving the rural districts without religious leadership. This had two effects: many rites fell into disuse and the people were driven back upon their own spiritual resources. Their ability to think and act religiously, separated from the mechanics of the Temple, was to be of very great value to them in the experience of the exile; but, on the other hand, many slipped back into irreligion as a result, so that Jeremiah became greatly discouraged over them (5:1-5).

With the religious life of the nation centered in Jerusalem, the Jerusalem priesthood established a monopoly of the nation's religion. In the matter of meat for food this was a very serious matter.

163   What did religion have to do with meat for food?

So long as the rural "high places" stood, it was a simple matter to take a sheep or a calf to the local shrine and have it slaughtered (see Question No. 9); but when they were destroyed, some provision had to be made for killing animals for food. The Book of the Law undertook to get around the difficulty (Deuteronomy

12:20-25) by giving the people the right to slaughter their animals "without benefits of clergy." The result was that eating meat ceased to have the religious significance it once had and the Temple altars became involved in a vicious system.

164 What was that vicious system that corrupted the altars?

Rural folk, going up to Jerusalem to perform their worship and offer their sacrifices, found it much more convenient to purchase the sacrificial beasts at the Temple, whereupon the authorities found it advantageous to go into the business of supplying animals for the sacrifices at a price that provided for a liberal profit. This paved the way for abuses which in Jesus' day had become an open scandal. When Jesus cleansed the Temple he attacked one of the most powerful rings of grafters in all the world (Matthew 21:12; Mark 11:15).

165 Was Jeremiah involved in Josiah's reforms?

Some scholars believe that two short sections (Jeremiah 8:8; 11:1-8, and possibly also 7:1-15; 11:15-16) refer to a conflict between the prophet and the Anathoth priests which resulted from Jeremiah's espousal of the reform party's program. This is a bit uncertain, but at least we know that he was bitterly disappointed over the results achieved by the reform.

166 Was the reform not successful?

The new rites and ceremonies did not alter the hearts of the people; their character remained unchanged. They attended the altars and offered their sacrifices to Yahweh but once they were outside the Temple they were at their evil deeds again. Obedience to the law was superficial and insincere (8:11). It did not change the underlying pattern of their lives; it only increased the prestige of the Temple (8:6). The Temple system, under the manipulation of the Temple priests, became a mockery; priests and people were alike unreliable; there was no sense of sins and no national conscience to which an appeal could be made. A noble instrument had failed.

167 How did the land reforms work?

It was asking too much of human nature to expect the rich to divide up with the poor even seven years. The reformers were inspired by a noble ideal, but they ignored human nature too much. It is extremely doubtful whether the whole system was ever actually put to work—at least there is no record of it having been done. But an event occurred which threw the whole scheme out of focus.

168 What happened?

With the fall of Nineveh the world was thrown into confusion, and in the brief interim between the destruction of Assyria and the consolidation of the power of Babylon, Egypt rushed to the assistance of Nineveh in the hope of checkmating Nebuchadrezzar. Josiah, going out to check Pharaoh Neco, was fatally wounded and brought home dead in his chariot (II Kings 23:29-30).

The death of Josiah was a terrible blow to the hopes of the "people's government"; but in a series of quick moves they were able to put Josiah's younger son, Jehoahaz, upon the throne in the faith that he would continue his father's policies and establish *mishpat*. His reign was short-lived, however. As Pharaoh Neco returned, he seized Jehoahaz, made him a prisoner, and put another son of Josiah upon the throne, giving him the name of Jehoiakim. Then he laid upon the tiny state an enormous tribute amounting to something like two and a half millions of dollars. And the worst feature of it was that the "people of the land"—the farmers and shepherds of the rural districts, *am ha'arets*—had to pay it (II Kings 23:33-35).

169 How did this affect the situation?

The pagan party in Jerusalem, after the few brief years under the radical government of the "people of the land," were now able to charge the prophetic party and the farmers with the responsibility of the nation's misfortunes. Moreover, with the kingdom under the necessity of paying tribute now to Egypt, the same conditions developed at the capital as had existed while the nation paid tribute to Assyria. In other words, the reactionaries came back into power and passed the tax load on to the rural landowners; Baal worship became popular and enjoyed the sanction of economic success. The religious worship remained centralized at the Temple, but only because it concentrated power in the hands of the municipal aristocracy of Jerusalem. Jehoiakim lost his head, plunged into a spending spree (Jeremiah 22:13-15, 18-19), and became a conceited fool who thought himself a great king over a powerful people, thus paving the way for his final overthrow.

170 What happened to the religious reforms?

The untimely death of Josiah raised a huge question mark in the minds of the people concerning the validity of the reforms he sponsored. Jeremiah's denunciations of the extravagances of Jehoiakim and his labor gangs were scathing and terrible (Jeremiah 22:13-15, 18-19), but not sufficient to create confidence in the minds of the people toward the religious reforms. As the prophet surveyed the scene he was almost ready to believe that there was not a single man in all the city who did *mishpat* (5:1). The revival of Baalism was attended by a loss of all the gains brought about by the Josiah reforms, and all this had the effect of bringing about a crisis in the prophet's thinking.

171 What was the nature of that crisis?

The popular religious doctrine generally believed throughout the East was to the effect that the good will of the gods was to be won by means of rites and ceremonies. Character as an accompaniment of religion was given no more than a passing thought. No one ever thought of winning the favor of a god by *being* something, but by *doing* something. The devout person was one who burned rams, sacrificed children, paid Temple dues, hired priests to offer prayers, and kept the rules of the shrine.

Against this whole concept the prophets through one hundred and fifty years had waged constant war. They had all recognized the futility of ceremonialism and had warned the nation that it was still a sinner, even though its ritual at the altars was perfect. But Jeremiah carried the thought one long step forward and insisted that good religion was a personal matter and not a national policy only—that personal character was the measure of true piety.

172 How could this be called a forward step?

Because Jeremiah was the first one of the prophets to make this a requirement. In the thinking of the earlier prophets the whole cause was national; the individual was thought of as a cell in the body of the state, and his responsibility was to the state. If the "cell" were righteous the state prospered, but if the "cell" were wicked the state suffered. The individual prospered or suffered along with the state.

Jeremiah transferred the whole matter of religion out of its social setting into an individual process. The individual gained as a result of piety or suffered as a result of wickedness, which meant that an individual might have the favor of God while the nation was under condemnation, or a person might be under the wrath of God at the same time that the nation was being favored. It was at this point that he broke with the prophetic party.

173 What was the issue between them?

The prophetic party sought to redeem the nation by destroying the "high places" and exalting the Temple at Jerusalem, in the belief that the nation would become righteous and favored by Yahweh if this could be accomplished. With fine patriotic fervor they appealed to the ancient law (Deuteronomy 18:21 ff.); but this to Jeremiah was little better than outright deception (Jeremiah 8:8 ff.), and from that time on there was no peace between the prophet and the party.

174 What was Jeremiah's concept?

He made the discovery that Moses had laid no such demands upon the people as the priests and prophets required. Instead, he had demanded faith and character on the part of individuals. Instead of emphasizing national righteousness, Jeremiah began emphasizing individual righteousness (31:33-34). This marked an entirely new epoch in religious thought: it meant that a man could actually be religious without any Temple and without any priest. This was revolutionary doctrine in such a time as that, and continues to be so even to our day. Jeremiah remembered that his own experience, whereby he came into his prophetic office, had not been any product of the Temple or of an altar, but that God had spoken to him in the midst of the quiet of Anathoth, far from smoking altars or burning sacrifices. Since Moses had not commanded any rites (7:22), Jeremiah concluded that God must have access to the heart of any individual at any time and that *the commands God laid upon individuals,* rather than the ceremonial requirements laid upon the nation, were the supreme law of life and of God. This was Jeremiah's great contribution to modern religion. It is commonplace to us, but it was a revolutionary step forward for the Hebrew of that day.

175 How was his idea accepted?

It suffered the fate of most new ideas in religion—it was rejected by the people of that generation, but it survived to become a cornerstone for our modern faith. But the point at which the prophet became most seriously involved was in his repudiation of Isaiah's doctrine of inviolability.

176 What was the inviolability controversy?

In the face of both the Scythian and the Babylonian crises Jeremiah believed the city of Jerusalem was in dire danger. He was persuaded that nothing could save it, because the nation was sinful; so he announced that God's favor had been alienated (7:4, 9-11, 13-15). At one of the feasts he preached a sermon in which he warned the people in the most solemn manner: "Amend your ways and your doings, and I will let you dwell in this place. Do not trust in these deceptive words: 'This is the temple of the Lord, the temple of the Lord.' . . . . Because you have done all these things, says the Lord, ... therefore I will do to the house which is called by my name, ... as I did to Shiloh. And I will cast you out of my sight, as I cast out all your kinsmen, all the offspring of Ephraim" (7:3-4, 13-15). Shiloh, where the ark of God was kept in the days of the judges, had not been saved from the Philistines (I Samuel 4); Ephraim was often used to mean all of Israel. The meaning then was plain; and for this daring speech Jeremiah might have been killed by the crowd except for the interference of some officers of the government.

177 How was he saved?

The people demanded that he be put to death; but the officers held a trial, at which the prophet Micah was quoted (Micah 3:12), and upon his authority Jeremiah was liberated. In this we get a glimpse of the continuing influence of the eighth-century prophets.

178 How did the political situation develop?

Jehoiakim, the son of Josiah, who was put upon the throne by Egypt, was an opportunist in politics as well as in religion, and his loyalties were always subject to suspicion. As a consequence Babylon, deciding to dispose of him, marched on Jerusalem with a considerable force. In the midst of the threat the king died and his son Jehoiachin succeeded him.

179 What was Jeremiah's relationship with Johoiakim?

Because of his opposition to the king's pro-Egyptian policy Jeremiah was quick to fall under royal disapproval. Moreover, Jehoiakim was generally disreputable (II Kings 23:37), his paganism, unreliability, and weak character making him appear contemptible in the sight of the prophet. The general effect was that Jeremiah's sermons were gloomy in the extreme. One day, in token of the fate awaiting the nation, in the midst of a sermon he broke a vessel of pottery into a thousand pieces (Jeremiah 19:11); and for his criticism of the government and the Temple he was beaten with rods and put into stocks, to all of which Jeremiah retaliated by forecasting the priest's speedy death (20:1-6).

On another occasion he saw a vessel in the potter's shop spoiled and a new one made of the same clay. This gave him the idea that a new nation would rise out of the ruins of the old (18:1 ff.) and another opportunity to preach the destruction of the old.

In the midst of the confusion which characterized the reign of Jehoiakim, Jeremiah decided on a bold stroke. He had been excluded from the Temple because of his affair with the priest (36:5), so he dictated a sermon and sent it by the hand of Baruch, his secretary, to be read aloud in the Temple. He had hoped to prevent a rebellion against Babylon, evidently believing that vassalage under Nebuchadrezzar was preferable to rebellion and destruction. Jehoiakim, the king, hearing of this affair, sent for Baruch and required that the book be read to him. As it was read he burned it, page by page, as a token of his contempt for the prophet (chapter 36). This led to an open break between Jeremiah and the king, and produced one of the most bitter denunciations of his prophetic career (22:13-19).

180 Did Jeremiah have the support of other religious leaders?

So far as the record goes there was no communication between Jeremiah and any of the other prophets whose writings appear in the Old Testament. We know nothing of his relations with Habakkuk, Nahum, or Zephaniah. Other prophets, however, were assuring the people that the nation was entering a period of unprecedented prosperity. These Jeremiah very frankly called frauds (23:17-21). One day, in a dramatic effort to symbolize the dreadful fate he believed was awaiting the nation, he appeared on the streets with a great wooden yoke about his neck. One of the false prophets engaged him in an argument and broke the yoke, declaring that his act in turn symbolized Yahweh's displeasure over Jeremiah's preaching. In reply Jeremiah assured the people that iron yokes would take the place of the wooden ones, and to make the cases more forceful he predicted that the prophet himself would die for the crime of telling the people a lie (28:2-14). Seven months thereafter the deceitful prophet was dead.

181 Was not Jeremiah a very lonely man?

The prophetic party deserted him because he did not support them in all their program. The priests repudiated him because he did not encourage the people to go to the Temple and support the rites and ceremonies. The people did not support him because he denied the doctrine of the inviolability of Jerusalem, a stand which cost him the confidence of the business interests of the capital. The government held him under suspicion because he was forever criticizing their foreign policy and predicting the destruction of Judah. By his own call to the ministry of prophecy he was denied the comforts and counsels of any normal family life. But out of all this loneliness Jeremiah developed his ideas of personal religion; thrown back upon himself through long hours of self-examination, he became conscious of the presence of Another—God seemed to speak to him directly and in person (17:9-10).

182 What happened to Jerusalem?

Jehoiakim's intrigues with Egypt having aroused the anger of Babylon, an army was sent to administer punishment. As they came on, the king died and his son Jehoiachin succeeded him.

He had been on the throne but three short months when the Babylonians besieged the city, compelled the young king to surrender, took more than ten thousand of the best mechanics and artisans captive, together with some priests and capitalists, and deported Jehoiachin in chains to Babylon. The queen mother made a vain attempt to save the situation by appealing personally to Nebuchadrezzar (II Kings 24:1 ff.), but in the end she shared the fate of her son.

The Babylonians had no desire to destroy the city. Their sole concern was that government should be in the hands of those whom they could trust to gather annual tribute and keep the peace. Zedekiah, the king's uncle, was given the chance; but he was an individual who itched for power. At the first opportunity, driven on by the landlords, he intrigued with Babylon's enemies and brought down upon the little nation again the whole wrath of the Empire (II Kings 25:1 ff.). For a time the wild desert tribes were permitted to ravage and despoil the villages; but after more pressing matters had been settled, Nebuchadrezzar loosed the dreadful might of the Babylonian armies. Jeremiah was appealed to in vain (Jeremiah 21:2-9); the city was sacked; Zedekiah was compelled to witness the killing of his own sons and then he was blinded. The Temple, the royal palace, the city walls—everything was destroyed and the bulk of the population carried off to Babylon as prisoners (II Kings 25:4-12).

183 What was Jeremiah doing all this time?

As a matter of principle he was opposed to revolt, and believed the nation's best interests would be served by accepting the Babylonian overlordship. At one time, in the midst of the siege, someone produced an ancient law that required the freeing of the slaves (Exodus 21:2; Deuteronomy 5:12); and the government, hard pressed by the foes without and terrified by the criticisms of the prophets inside the walls, decided that the law should be obeyed. Perhaps, after all, if they freed their slaves Yahweh might help them. But a few weeks afterward, when their military fortunes had improved a bit, the luckless slaves were thrust back into their slavery again (Jeremiah 34:11). This affair called forth one of Jeremiah's bitterest speeches (34:12-21).

His advocacy of acceptance of the Babylonian yoke made him extremely unpopular with the government, of course, and with many of the people, particularly the landlords who had most to lose. As he was leaving the city one day on an innocent errand he was seized and charged with conniving with the enemy. It was declared that he was slipping out of the city for the purpose of betraying it into the hands of the invader (37:13). This accusation he denied, of course; but no one would listen to his defense, and he was cast into a dungeon (37:15; 38:6). A Negro slave managed his release (38:7-13), and immediately he began preaching again, the experience in no wise softening his message or his words (37:17-20).

One day, in the midst of the siege, a cousin arrived with an offer to sell to him a piece of land which had belonged to Jeremiah's family estate. It was about the worst possible time in which to buy land, but in the presence of a large number of witnesses the prophet made the purchase and placed the deed in a safe place as testimony to his faith that sometime there would be a restoration (32:6-15). This hope he expressed best, perhaps, in his messages to the exiles.

184 Who were those exiles?

It will be remembered that two crowds of exiles were carried away—one in 597 B.C. and one in 586 B.C. It was to the first company that Jeremiah wrote.

Those who were left in the land assumed they were better favored of Yahweh than were the captives, and they looked with contempt on the prisoners (Ezekiel 11:5). But in a vigorous sermon Jeremiah declared them to be the flower of the nation and the hope of the future (Jeremiah 24:1-10). This of course did not add to his popularity at home. In his message to the exiles, however, he warned against any hope for a speedy return (29:4 ff.) and advised them to put their trust in Yahweh (29:12-15). Certain prophets who were carried off with the first batch of exiles were enraged when they heard this letter read in Babylon and sent back a demand that the authorities in Jerusalem should silence him, to which Jeremiah replied in a stinging rebuke (29:26-32).

185 Was Jeremiah ever taken captive?

There seems to be some reason to believe that the Babylonians knew about his activities, for they treated him kindly. Perhaps in the minds of many of his countrymen he was viewed as a "fifth columnist." But at any rate after the city was destroyed he began preaching to the scattered remnants of the nation that Yahweh would rebuild the walls of the city for them, in time, and that they would become the nucleus of the new community if they would accept their responsibilities bravely and remain in Jerusalem, living righteously (42:10 ff.). This attracted the attention of some of the leaders and they sought his advice, only to involve him in more difficulty.

186 What more could he suffer?

The people who were left behind were put under the authority of a high-minded governor named Gedaliah. Jeremiah believed in him and set about to assist him in rebuilding the life of the poor little stricken state. Some progress was being made when, without warning or provocation, the governor was murdered by some member of the royal family who had been accidentally overlooked by the Babylonians. This crime frightened the people and they fully expected some new blow, and it was at this juncture that they turned to Jeremiah for advice. After studying the matter for ten days he announced that it was Yahweh's plan that they should stay with the land and face the situation, taking their chances with Nebuchadrezzar. Disregarding his counsel they decided on a hurried flight into Egypt, whereupon they seized Jeremiah and compelled him to accompany them to Egypt (42:1—43:7). There he was kept, virtually a prisoner, by his own countrymen.

187 What was Jeremiah's fate in Egypt?

The fleeing Hebrews settled first on the eastern edge of the Nile Delta, though a small party made its way farther south. The wrecking of the nation, the destruction of the state, the blinding and imprisonment of their king, and the misery of the people had the effect of destroying their faith in Yahweh. In Egypt therefore they turned to the worship of the "Queen of Heaven," a religion that had had some vogue in Palestine previous to the reign of Josiah. This defection called for a bold rebuke from Jeremiah, who insisted that all their troubles had been caused by their apostasy and that this new spiritual treason would certainly lead to further disaster. But the people laughed him to scorn. Thus, left alone, he contends for the ancient faith of his people in one of the most impressive messages of his entire book (chapter 44).

188 What was the outcome?

No one knows. At this point Jeremiah disappears from the scene. Tradition declares that he suffered martyrdom, but there is no positive historical evidence to prove it. The Hebrews who were carried to Babylon became the progenitors of the new Judaism; and to them, rather than to the Egyptian group, we owe our modern faith. It was in the Exile that Hebrew religion made it greatest progress.

189 When did Jeremiah write his book?

It will be remembered that at one time he sent his secretary, Baruch, to read his message to King Jehoiakim, and that the king burned it page by page. When this was reported to Jeremiah he immediately sat down and wrote an enlarged and more complete edition which is, according to the belief of scholars, the major portion of his book as we have it in our Bible today (chapter 36 and Question No. 179).

190 What was Jeremiah's great contribution to religion?

His ministry was so long and varied, he met so many issues and discussed so many matters, that it is hard to condense his message into the space of a few sentences; but his major ideas can be enumerated in a few simple points.

1. He believed in God's universal authority. He saw every nation used by God for the accomplishment of some great ideal. No state or people were outside his plans.

2. He had found God outside the Temple without the aid of rite or ceremony, and thenceforth believed any other man could do the same thing. Religion was, to him, the most personal and real experience of life.

3. In his counsel to the exiles he urged that they should build their religious life independent of the Temple and of the Hebrew state. This was a revolutionary doctrine, for no god existed anywhere in the world without a state to support him. To worship Yahweh in Babylon, with Jerusalem and the Temple

in ruins and the government of Judah destroyed, was a startling proposal. It may be a commonplace to us, but that is because Jeremiah pioneered the idea.

4. He believed in an ultimate restoration of Judah as a spiritual state, with a divine and spiritual destiny. For that reason he contended with the politicians because they stood in the way of the achievement of this great spiritual destiny of the people.

5. He believed the law of Yahweh was written upon the consciences of individual men rather than upon the books of the law. This belief was a forerunner of the later Christian doctrine to the effect that the Holy Spirit spoke to each believer, and this in turn was of great significance to the Protestant movement which took the position that all believers were members of the priesthood and had equal access to the heart and mind of God. Jeremiah was opposed to all legalism in religion and sought with all his ability to promote personal religion and upbuild personal religious convictions among the people.

6. He believed that every king and government was responsible to God for the welfare of the people, and should be a moral example to save the nation from sinning. As a prophet he maintained the right to rebuke kings, politicians, nobles, and priests in the name of God. He had no economic theory to advance; he was in no wise responsible for the impossible land laws suggested by Deuteronomy; he was in every sense an independent thinker. His greatest assets were (1) powerful convictions and (2) the courage to voice them.

In the midst of danger he was brave. In the midst of trouble he was true. In the midst of confusion he was calm. In the midst of the dark he was a flame. Under all circumstances he set a standard for the prophets who followed him. And because of his great reputation as a speaker for God he was credited with the authorship of a book which he probably never saw.

191 What book is that?

The book of Lamentations in the Old Testament.

192 What is the book of Lamentations?

It is a collection of five Hebrew poems, each complete in itself, and each expressing a common emotion—profound grief. All are written in that form of Hebrew poetry which was commonly used on the occasion of funerals, and each may be described as a dirge.

193 When were they written?

In no case does any poem give the precise date of its composition. It is necessary to study the contents of each to determine the matter; and such a study reveals the fact that all were inspired by the sufferings of the Hebrew people at or about the time of the destruction of Jerusalem.

194 What were the circumstances?

The Babylonian Empire, as has been stated, had no desire to destroy the small states, for they produced less revenue when devasted than when intact, and the Empire was interest in revenue in the form of tribute. It was happy to leave them undisturbed so long as they paid the taxes regularly and fully. It was only when they defied the Empire and undertook to escape the payment of the tribute that the terrible might of Babylon was loosed upon them, and then they were reduced to impotency.

It had been Zedekiah's revolt which had brought the Babylonian hosts up to the walls of Jerusalem. The king had surrounded himself with a crowd of disreputables whom Jeremiah called "bad figs" (Jeremiah 24), an expression somewhat similar to the modern slang "bad eggs." This deluded crowd in 588 B.C. persuaded Zedekiah to raise the standard of revolt, the question of taxes being at the bottom of the whole matter.

The Hebrews have always been a difficult people to enslave. There was something in their religion which taught them that they were made in the image of God, and this concept of their own dignity unfitted them for slavery. In Jesus' day the Jew on the auction block brought the lowest price of any man offered for sale, because he was a notoriously poor slave.

Though the government of Babylon was reasonably generous as tyrannies go, the Hebrews were a yeasty people, always ready for revolt, and the patience of Nebuchadrezzar was scant. When he took up the gage of battle he was determined to see it through to a finish that would not be forgotten.

The stubborn resistance and astounding courage of the Hebrews in defending their beautiful capital have inspired historians to this day. Their ability to hold out against overwhelming odds in spite of the horrors of a terrible siege was simply amazing. For almost two years the beleagured city absorbed the most staggering blows the Babylonian hosts could deal. Shut in behind their massive walls, almost entirely dependent upon the occasional rain for their water supply, manning their walls day and night, confronted by every engine of war that ancient ingenuity could devise, nursing their wounded week after week without relief, shut off from all but the most meager food supplies, unable to replenish their stores of clothing, every man, woman, and child gave his last ounce of strength and effort to the city's defense. But their cause was hopeless from the beginning, and on the fourth day of the eighteenth month of the siege the walls were breached, the enemy poured through like a tide of white-hot lava, and within the hour the city was a shambles.

195 How are these poems related to these events?

They are descriptions of the sufferings of the people, the terror of the fleeing king and army, the horrors of the siege and the slaughter of the inhabitants, the final leveling of the city, and at least one (Lamentations 5) seems to be a valiant defense of the good name of the aristocracy of Jerusalem which has borne the brunt of the disaster.

196 Who wrote them?

No one knows. The poet nowhere identifies himself. But they seem to have been written by an eyewitness of the events described, for few could have penned such passionate lines unless they had seen the terrible drama as it was being enacted; no one could have written so vivid an account without having lived the horrors that are described. The most we can say with certainty is that they are the work of some master, or masters, of Hebrew poetry who wrote under the inspiration of death, pain, torture, horror, and devastating grief.

197 Could Jeremiah have written them?

It would be impossible to say he could not have written them, though it is not likely. He must have witnessed the destruction of the city, and certainly he lays the blame for that tragedy at the feet of the rulers as does the poet; but in various passages (for example, 1:21-22; 2:9, 14; 3:59-66; 4:13, 20) these poems express ideas that seem hardly likely to have come from the pen of the same prophet who composed Jeremiah's known sermons.

198 Is he not credited with them?

In most versions of the Bible they bear the title "The Lamentations of Jeremiah," because the first poem once had an introduction connecting them with Jeremiah; but it is known that this was added by the Greek translators of Alexandria about 200 B.C. They also gave the book its name, "Lamentations." We must remember that the original collection had no name, and that the name of Jeremiah did not appear in the collection in any way.

199 Were they all written by the same author?

Again we must say that we do not know. There are those who believe that each was written by a different author and that the five were assembled in one collection because of their common theme. There are others who believe they are all the product of the inspiration of one poetical genius. The question is not important, for the significance of none of them, unless it be the last, is in any way dependent upon the identity of the author.

200 What about the last poem?

It has much to say about the nobles, the elders, and the leaders, which gives some reason to believe that the author was a member of the aristocracy and was particularly interested in defending their memory. And it is worth remembering that the aristocracy was centered in Jerusalem and must have suffered with especial severity during the siege.

201 Does the poetical form appear in the Bible?

The King James Version, with which the average reader is most familiar, does not print poetry in its proper poetical form; but in the Revised Standard Version and other recent versions this form does appear very plainly.

202 Was such poetry common among the Hebrews?

Some of the earlier Hebrew poems are dirges sung on the

occasion of a great sorrow or tragedy. David composed one such when Saul and Jonathan were killed in battle (II Samuel 1:19-27); and Amos lapsed into a dirge (5:1-2) in the midst of his address at Bethel, speaking as though he were presiding over Israel's funeral.

203 What does the first poem have to say?

In a mood of deep penitence, the author speaks in the name of the nation and confesses its sins. He freely admits that the awful punishment was well deserved, but he prays that Judah's enemies may also be punished.

204 What about the second poem?

It is easy to believe that the second and fourth poems were written by someone who escaped with Zedekiah on that first terrible day when the Babylonians, having broken through the walls at last, were killing, destroying, burning, and devastating the city. The terrible scenes of those last days were before his mind—the pitiful cries of the little children, the haggard faces of the men, the awful eyes of the women, mothers eating the flesh of their own children—all this and more he poured into the livid lines which describe those last terrible hours in the capital.

205 What about the third poem?

This is the well-known acrostic form of poetry, less moving than the others, and it may have been written somewhat farther from the scene of the catastrophe.

206 What about the fifth poem?

There seems to be good reason to believe this was written some time after the destruction of Jerusalem, probably by some aristocratic poet among the exiles. He presents the pitiful case of the people, especially the aristocracy, and begs for mercy in their behalf. The style of his poem is a little different from the others, the lines being much abbreviated; but the same pathetic quality which appears in the other four is apparent in the fifth.

207 Does this complete the literature of this period?

It is well known that other literature was produced, and some of it appears in the Old Testament in other books; but in the six books described in this study we have the only complete compositions which came to their present form during these dreadful decades. In many ways it was one of the most significant centuries, and certainly the most tragic, in Hebrew history. Hereafter the fate of Judaism is in the keeping of exiles who are captives.